CAPITALISM, THE FAMILY, & PERSONAL LIFE

STATE AND REVOLUTION

THE CORPORATIONS AND THE STATE
Essays in the Theory of Capitalism and Imperialism
James O'Connor

THE MAFIA OF A SICILIAN VILLAGE, 1860–1960:
A Study of Violent Peasant Entrepreneurs
Anton Blok

ELI ZARETSKY

CAPITALISM, THE FAMILY, & PERSONAL LIFE

HARPER TORCHBOOKS
Harper & Row, Publishers
New York, Cambridge, Philadelphia, San Francisco
London, Mexico City, São Paulo, Sydney

This book was first published in Great Britain in 1976 by
Pluto Press Limited. It originally appeared as a series of
articles in *Socialist Revolution*, nos. 13–15, January–June
1973.

First HARPER PAPERBACK edition published 1976.

LIBRARY OF CONGRESS CATALOG CARD NUMBER: 76–21168

ISBN 0-06-131972-4

82 83 84 85 86 10 9

To my parents

Contents

Preface

The following book examines the division between the private and public, or inner and outer worlds of our society. It explains this division in terms of the impact of capitalism upon the family: on one hand, the decline of the traditional patriarchal family, based upon private productive property; on the other, the rise of a new emphasis on personal life, experienced as something outside work and society.

Chapter 1 shows how the contemporary women's movement discovered, but did not challenge, the idea that the economy and the family are two separate and autonomous realms.

Chapter 2 argues that this dichotomy is specific to capitalist society, and that the two realms must be seen as one integrated system. Chapter 2 also contains an overview of the historical material which follows.

Chapter 3 traces the meaning which the family has had in capitalist society, and shows how this meaning has been rooted in the family's changing place in the system of production. It traces the process by which each succeeding historical class – aristocracy, bourgeoisie, working class – both perpetuated and transformed the familial and personal ideals of its predecessors.

Chapter 4 puts forth the underlying thesis of the book. It argues that the rise of industrial capitalism, while destroying the traditional form of family life, gave rise to a new search for personal identity which takes place outside the division of labour. In a phrase: proletarianization gave rise to subjectivity. Many distinctively modern trends from the 'child-centred' family to romantic art to an emphasis on sexuality all reflect this development. While the rise of industry largely freed women from traditional patriarchal constraints, the expansion of personal life created a new basis for their oppression – the responsibility for maintaining a private refuge from an impersonal society.

Chapter 5 surveys the various modern movements that have sought to transform the family – utopian and Marxian socialism, the Russian and Chinese revolutions, feminism, bohemia and cultural radicalism – and shows how they have all reflected, in their own thinking and practice, the underlying dichotomy in the society.

Chapter 6 examines the relevance of psychoanalysis to this subject.

A brief appendix discusses the political implications of the analysis.

While writing this work I was immersed in the intense political atmosphere of the San Francisco Bay Area – the socialist currents that have supplanted the new left, an extremely diverse and vigorous feminist movement, and *Socialist Revolution* magazine for which this work was first conceived and written (and which first published it as a series of articles, January–June 1973). I believe that my greatest debt is to this political ferment, and the rethinking which I went through, particularly under the stimulus of the women's movement, is one which I know I have shared with many people. Certain individuals, however, played a special role.

My friend and co-worker on *Socialist Revolution*, John Judis, encouraged me from the first, shared his ideas fully and generously over a period of years, and edited, re-edited, and continued to re-edit the final version, until he felt that it was as good as I and he could accomplish.

Largely because this was my first work, its writing was a profound, and often painful ordeal. My wife, Linda Zaretsky, lived this ordeal with me and helped me to go beyond it. As part of this help, she read all of its versions, made countless suggestions, almost all of which I heeded, and continually tried to force my attention onto the real questions, personal and political, that were at stake.

Many of the ideas in this work can be ultimately traced to decade-old conversations with Martin J. Sklar, who first convinced me of the relevance of socialism to our society. I have also drawn deeply from his published work, particularly 'On the Proletarian Revolution and the End of Political-Economic Society' (*Radical America*, May 1969).

I wish also to thank the Louis M. Rabinowitz Foundation for its generous support, Ruth Bloch for several suggestions of major importance, Don Jelinek, Gil Weisman, the Socialist Revolution collective and, finally, for reasons that I cannot really put into words, my four year old daughter, Tasha.

1.
Feminism and Socialism

The women's liberation movement, since its emergence in the late 1960s, has posed a series of fundamental challenges to traditional socialist politics. Against the emphasis on the industrial proletariat it raised the needs of women in the home and children, the majority of the population. Against the emphasis on capitalism, women's liberation attacked male supremacy, a form of oppression that certainly antedated capitalism and that has persisted in the socialist countries. Women's liberation promised to go beyond what it regarded as the narrowly economic perspective of socialists in order to revolutionize the deepest and most universal experiences of life – those of 'personal' relations, love, egotism, sexuality, our inner emotional lives. Just as socialists in the nineteenth century had challenged bourgeois liberal politics by rejecting its exclusive focus on the state and by raising the importance of economic relations, so feminists brought into the arena of political discussion the hitherto private life of the family.

The early writings of the women's movement were fragmentary and exploratory, symbolized by the well-worn, mimeographed articles that for several years were the movement's basic texts. The first attempt at an overall synthesis came in 1970 with the publication of Kate Millett's *Sexual Politics*, which the author described as 'something of a pioneering effort . . . tentative and imperfect'.[1] *Sexual Politics*, as its title indicates, was an attempt to broaden the meaning of politics. It began with an analysis of how three modern novelists had dealt with sexual intercourse: 'Coitus of itself appears a biological and physical activity', wrote Millett, but in fact it is a social act, 'a charged microcosm of the variety of attitudes and values to which culture subscribes'. Sexual encounters had political meaning since they involved 'power-structured relationships . . . whereby one group of persons is controlled by another'. Millett sought to broaden the meaning of politics to include power relationships of 'personal contact and interaction between members of well-defined and coherent groups'.[2]

Millett's concern was with male supremacy, the most pervasive of these power relationships. She argued that male supremacy, which presented itself as a natural or biological phenomenon, was in fact socially enforced through ideological conditioning, socialization of early childhood, restriction of women to the family, the male monopoly on violence, and other institutions. Through such means women were universally subordinated to men. While Millett did not draw explicit political conclusions, her book encouraged the idea that a feminist movement primarily concerned with the abolition of male supremacy in both its social and 'personal' manifestations was needed.

Insisting that male supremacy was a social rather than a biological phenomenon, *Sexual Politics* reflected the early stage of women's liberation: the first priority was to establish the validity of its concern. But while describing various ways in which male supremacy operated, Millett did not present a unified theory of male supremacy. As Juliet Mitchell later wrote: 'We are left with a sense of the random and chaotic and *equal* contribution of each and all to the maintenance of patriarchy'.[3] Millett did not explain what gave rise to male supremacy in the first place nor why, if male supremacy was socially established, it was universally reproduced while other

14

social institutions varied throughout history. Without such an explanation it was impossible for Millett to outline a strategy for ending male supremacy.

About a year later an explanation was attempted in Shulamith Firestone's *The Dialectic of Sex* (1970), probably the major single statement of radical feminist theory to date. Firestone's great innovation was in accepting the traditional view that it was 'natural' for men to rule women, and turning the implications of this fact on their heads. While Firestone agreed with Millett that male supremacy was socially enforced, she insisted that its origins arose before society in the 'biological family' – 'the basic reproductive unit of male/female/-infant'. According to Firestone, this is a form of life that dates back to our animal beginnings and persists in the most developed society. As a result of their child-rearing function (and infancy lasts much longer among humans than among other animal species) women have always been at the 'mercy of their biology'. The 'biological family' has been the cell, the basic social unit, 'everywhere, throughout time'. As society developed, women remained restricted to the family, while men went forth to organize production, politics, and war. Society was divided into 'two distinct biological classes' unequal in their social roles. This class division underlies all subsequent history. Explicitly rejecting the marxist view that the class struggle originates in the 'economic development of society' and 'in changes of the modes of production and exchange', Firestone urged us to seek 'the ultimate cause and the great moving power of all historic events in the dialectic of sex'.

In accord with this theory, Firestone tried to show that radical feminism would subsume the major political grievances of our time: economic inequality, race, ecology, etc. The fundamental social imbalance of power that characterizes the

15

biological family – women dependent on men, children dependent on adults – has given rise to a 'power psychology', a 'psychological pattern of dominance-submission'. This ceaseless striving for power shapes our most intimate personal relations (Firestone analyses the 'unequal power' struggle of romantic love) as well as the major transformations of world history.[4] Political movements that attack outward forms of oppression such as racism or capitalism without transforming the family merely skim the surface of society.

Having offered an explanation for the origins of male supremacy, Firestone was able to outline a strategic programme for ending it. While male supremacy had originated in nature, it was possible to end it through new technology – contraception and the possibility of producing children outside the womb. The opportunity, she wrote, is finally at hand for men and women to 'outgrow nature'. But the opportunity must be seized and carried through by a feminist movement.

Firestone's book, along with other products of the women's movement, crystallized many people's dissatisfaction with the traditional politics of the left. Socialism, staking all on a reorganization of the economy, appeared inadequate to the needs of modern men and women. Socialism promised to revolutionize society on the basis of narrow programmes that did not touch the inner life of people. Firestone's book spoke to the deep distrust of both bourgeois and radical politics that prevails in our society. Politics promises to affect us in what we share with large numbers of people, but in much of our lives we feel unique or alone. Firestone's stress on the importance of the family evoked a new conception of a political movement: one that would make the inner emotional life of its participants part of its practice. Within the women's movement in this period small 'consciousness raising' groups spread with incredible vitality and vigour. Elsewhere on the left this was a period in

16

which collectives, communes, men's groups, radical therapy, and other attempts to integrate personal and political life flourished. Many male radicals now saw in women's liberation the possibility of a new kind of revolutionary movement.

Firestone was able to advance the early attack on male supremacy by pointing to a specific institution that caused it – the family. This gave a concrete – or, as Firestone said, 'materialist' – basis to a phenomenon whose very omnipresence made it appear psychologically determined. By focusing on the family, Firestone was able to relate two separate questions – the oppression of women and the place of personal experience within society – in new and exciting ways. The family *is* the primary institution through which women participate in this society. While Firestone ignored the important fact that women also work outside the home, even working women give the family their primary allegiance. Wherever a woman is in this society, it is the family, and the ideology of the family, that contributes most to shaping her beliefs and maintaining her oppression. In addition, the family is the institution in which one's personal uniqueness is central. It is the crucible in which our emotional life first takes shape and throughout life is the major institution in our society in which we expect to be recognized and cared for, for ourselves. Men, and, to a lesser degree, women, gain a social identity through school or work. But even as adults our 'personal' life is confined to the family or to relationships – friendships, love affairs, communal life – that closely resemble it or are based upon it.

Firestone tied the liberation of women to an attack on the family. In *The Dialectic of Sex* she distinguished radical feminism, which directly attacked the 'sexual class system', from other tendencies: 'conservative feminists' (who 'concentrate on the more superficial symptoms of sexism – legal inequities, employment discrimination, and the like'),

17

'politicos', 'ladies' Auxiliaries of the Left', etc.[5] But in practice the focus on the family and personal relations has proved an insufficient basis for a political movement. During 1971, 'consciousness raising' small groups, the most widespread practice of radical feminism, began to decline partly because they could not cohere into an organized movement and partly because of their limitations in helping their members resolve their 'personal' problems. Radical lesbianism advanced the attack on the family by urging women to break completely with their 'female role' – in love, in living arrangements, and in sexuality. But radical lesbianism also showed how a political focus on the family and personal relations could lead away from building a social movement and toward entirely personal transformations. Firestone's equation of women's oppression with their oppression within the family obscured the special problems of black and brown women, and of industrial working class women. The idea that male supremacy could be ended through an attack on the intimate personal relations of the family alone began to decline. Similarly, small groups and communes began to give way or go back to political action projects which sought public power (over day care, welfare, women's health, etc.) while maintaining a commitment to personal transformation.

The women's movement's next major advance in the critique of the family, Juliet Mitchell's *Women's Estate* (1971), explained many of the limitations in the radical feminist perspective as presented by Firestone. While it was written from English experience, Mitchell's book has an internationalist perspective and raises problems shared by the diverse feminist movements in the developed capitalist countries. Both Millett and Firestone are socialists, but they see the relevance of socialism only in relation to strictly economic questions. Mitchell, on the other hand, urges that we develop a socialist theory of women's oppression and of the family: 'We should ask the feminist questions, but try to come up with some Marxist answers.'[6] Mitchell criticized Millett's concept of patriarchy as a universal political system: 'a political system is dependent upon (a part of) a specific mode of production: patriarchy, though a perpetual feature of it, is not in *itself* a mode of production, though an essential aspect of every economy, it does not dominantly determine it.'[7] Similarly, Mitchell criticized Firestone's account as ahistorical. While praising Firestone for giving 'full weight to the objective physiological sexual differences', she wrote:

> To say that sex dualism was the first oppression and that it underlies all oppression may be true, but it is a general, non-specific truth, it is simplistic materialism, no more. After all we can say there has always been a master class and a servant class, but it does matter *how* these function (whether they are feudal landlords and peasants, capitalists and the working class or so on); there have always been classes, as there have always been sexes, how do these operate within any given, specific society?[8]

Mitchell's contribution to the analysis of women's oppression falls into two parts. The first, largely a reprint of her 1966 article 'Women: The Longest Revolution', analyses the historic failure of the socialist movement to deal with the oppression of women. Mitchell traces this failure to an abstract conception of the family – a 'hypostatized entity' she calls it – and she quotes Marx approvingly: 'One cannot, in general, speak of the family "as such".'[9] Mitchell urged that we resolve the family into the separate 'structures' that compose it: sexuality, reproduction, and socialization of the young. These three structures had been condensed within the apparent monolith of the family, which was then portrayed ideologically as a 'natural' institution within which women performed 'natural' functions: sex, childbirth, and the rearing of children. Mitchell agreed with Firestone that the root of the oppression of women was their exclusion from production and their restriction to the family. The way out, for Mitchell, was not to attack the 'family' but to differentiate the structures that compose it. Hence, Mitchell urged revolutionaries to develop a complex, coordinated programme for the separate structures that defined women's condition: sexuality, reproduction, socialization, and production (by which Mitchell meant socialized production, outside the family). She emphasized that these structures were interconnected so that while birth control, for example, had reduced the weight of reproduction in maintaining the oppression of women, this had been offset by the increased attention paid to socialization. But she did not explain how the unity of the family had been constituted nor how the 'triptych' of familial functions ('the woman's world') was, as she put it, 'embraced by production (the man's world) – precisely a structure that in the final instance is determined by the economy'.[10]

The later sections of *Women's Estate* address themselves to this problem. Mitchell describes the unity of the family in three ways. First, it is always formed as an economic unit. In the present, for example, it serves as a means of reproducing the labour force and as an arena of consumption. This economic dimension constantly varies throughout history and is directly dependent upon the mode of production. Second, the family's unity is formed ideologically – for the contemporary family the key idea is private property, a feudal (and early bourgeois) ideal that, like all ideology, 'preserves itself across revolutionary changes in the mode of production'. The family encapsulates the 'most conservative concepts available'.[11] Finally, Mitchell explains the relative autonomy of the family from history by its 'biosocial' form –

the basic mother/father/child relationship that Firestone had made central. In this relationship, within the family, the 'human animal' is 'socially constructed' and male supremacy first takes shape. In the universal repetition of basic patterns of early childhood – which Freud had described as the oedipus complex – the anatomical differences between men and women are given their social meaning. Mitchell urged the value of psychoanalysis for studying 'the borderline between the biological and the social, which finds expression in the family' and concluded:

> The bio-social universal, the ideological atemporal, the economic specificity all interlock in a complex manner.... Psychoanalysis, the scientific method for investigating the first [the bio-social], can be neglected no more than scientific socialism for understanding the last, the economic, and both are needed for developing a comprehension of the ideological. [12]

Radical feminism, as represented by Firestone, had stressed the role of the family in determining the nature of society. Mitchell advanced this perspective by demonstrating that society simultaneously formed the family. Mitchell also showed us how deep and difficult these problems are. But in one respect her account preserved the dualism that characterized Firestone's account. She described the family as divided between its objective economic functions (formed by capitalism) and its inner psychological life (arising from male supremacy as embodied in the oedipus complex), she then posited an intermediate realm – the 'ideological' – in which economic and psychological life interact. But this severely limits the value of what Mitchell called for earlier in her book: 'the use of scientific socialism as a method of analysing the specific nature of [women's] oppression.'[13] It restricts marxism to the study of economic and ideological activity, and excludes from marxist analysis areas of life that are critical to an understanding of women's oppression and of social life generally – the emotions, sexuality, infancy and childhood, and the instinctual life of both sexes, as well as such 'bio-social' processes as ageing, sickness, and death. Instead of expanding marxism to include these areas of life (and using the discoveries of psychoanalysis to do this) Mitchell left marxism in its traditional place and introduced psychoanalysis as a residual category to deal with the problems marxists have slighted. Mitchell's formulation threatened to reproduce the very dichotomy between socialism (the economy) and feminism (the family) that she criticised so well. It is clear from Mitchell's rich account that a revolutionary movement that takes seriously the task of ending male supremacy and of transforming psychological life must be variegated and must operate on many different levels at once. But if socialist analysis is not adequate, what principles could unify such a movement?

2.
The Family and the Economy

According to Firestone, both the oppression of women and the split in society between intimate personal experience and anonymous social relations are consequences of the sexual division of labour within the family. Firestone terms the family the base and the political economy the superstructure, but links the two realms only vaguely through 'power psychology'. While Mitchell stresses the complexity of their interaction she retains the conception of the family as a separate realm (socially defined as 'natural') outside the economy – indeed she explains the oppression of women, as Firestone does, by their exclusion from social production.* In this way, Mitchell and Firestone share with recent socialist movements the idea of a split between the family and the economy. Given this idea, one cannot understand the relation between family life and the rest of society.

The understanding of the family and the economy as separate realms is specific to capitalist society. By the 'economy', Firestone and Mitchell mean the sphere in which commodity production and exchange takes place, the production of goods

---

* In an exchange over 'The Longest Revolution' Mitchell wrote that the roles performed by women within the family – sexuality, reproduction, and socialization – were all 'roles man shares with other mammals. This confirms de Beauvoir's contention that women are relegated to the species while men – through work – transcend it.' *New Left Review* 41, p.82.

and services to be sold, and their sale and purchase. Within this framework of thought, a housewife cooking a meal is not performing economic activity, whereas if she were hired to cook a similar meal in a restaurant she would be. This conception of 'economic' excludes activity within the family and a political struggle waged by 'economic classes' would exclude women, except in their role as wage-earners. Socialist and communist movements in the developed capitalist countries have also understood the 'economy' in this way. And when they have talked of a political struggle between 'economic classes', they have essentially excluded both the family and housewives from revolutionary politics.

The historic socialist understanding is based upon an important truth about capitalist society. The capitalist class has organized much of material production as a system of commodity production and exchange, and has organized most forms of labour as wage labour – i.e., as a commodity. By paying the labourer less than the value that the labourer produces, the capitalist is able to appropriate surplus value, unpaid labour time. Surplus value is the social basis for the existence of the capitalist class. The sphere in which surplus value is produced and realized (the 'economy') determines the imperatives of society as a whole. The family has changed in capitalist society as the needs generated within the sphere of surplus value production – the needs of the capitalist class – have changed. And since this sphere is organized through wage labour, the destruction of the wage labour system is a central, defining task of a revolutionary movement in a capitalist country. But this task cannot be accomplished by wage labour alone, nor does it exhaust the purposes of a revolutionary movement.

The organization of production in capitalist society is predicated upon the existence of a certain form of family life. The wage labour system socialized production under capitalism) is sustained by the socially necessary but private labour of housewives and mothers. Child-rearing, cleaning, laundry, the maintenance of property, the preparation of food, daily health care, reproduction, etc. constitute a perpetual cycle of labour necessary to maintain life in this society. In this sense the family is an integral part of the economy under capitalism. Furthermore, the functions currently performed by housewives and mothers will be as indispensable to a socialist society as will be many of the forms of material production currently performed by wage labour. A socialist movement that anticipates its own role in organizing society must give weight to all forms of socially necessary labour, rather than only to the form (wage labour) that is dominant under capitalism.

Marx probably intended the larger conception of the economy when, in the preface to the *Critique of Political Economy*, he defined the 'economic structure' as the 'real foundation' of society. The 'economic structure', he wrote, was 'the total ensemble of social relations entered into in the social production of existence.' That this conception of economic structure must include the family would have been perfectly clear in any analysis of a pre-capitalist society.* In

---

* By the 'family' I mean any grouping of parents or other relatives with children, embodying a sexual division of labour, and distinguishing itself as a unit by legal, economic, and sexual rights and taboos. While such a unit varies endlessly in form, constitution, and relationship to other social institutions, it is also more or less universal in human societies (though not among all strata of a given society). The best introduction I know to the conception of the family as an anthropological (i.e., universal) entity is Claude Levi-Strauss, 'The Family', in Arlene and Jerome Skolnick, *Family in Transition*, Boston 1971.

pre-capitalist society the family performed such present functions as reproduction, care of the sick and aged, shelter, the
maintenance of personal property, and regulation of sexuality, as well as the basic forms of material production necessary to sustain life. There were forms of economic activity
that were not based upon family units – such as the building
of public works, and labour in state-owned mines or industries. But they do not compare in extent or importance to
peasant agriculture, labour based upon some form of the
family, or upon the village, an extension of one or several
families. In the most 'primitive' societies – those in which
production is least developed socially – the material necessity
of the family, its role in sustaining life, was overwhelming.
Even putting aside the dependence of children, adults in
'primitive' society had no option but to rely upon the cooperative work of the household and particularly on the sexual
division of labour, which by restricting tasks to one sex or the
other insured their reciprocal dependence. In such societies,
widows, orphans, and bachelors are scorned or pitied as if
they were witches or cripples: their survival is always in
doubt.*

It is only under capitalism that material production organized as wage labour and the forms of production taking
place within the family, have been separated so that the 'econ-

---

* Claude Levi-Strauss described 'meeting, among the Bororo of
central Brazil, a man about thirty years old: unclean, ill-fed, sad,
and lonesome. When asked if the man were seriously ill, the natives'
answer came as a shock: what was wrong with him? – nothing at all,
he was just a bachelor. [Since] only the married status permits the
man to benefit from the fruits of women's work, including delousing,
body-painting, and hair-plucking as well as vegetable food and
cooked food . . . a bachelor is really only half a human being'. 'The
Family', p. 57.

omic' function of the family is obscured. Both Firestone and Mitchell contrast the 'natural' functions of the family to the more 'human' world of social production, but sexuality and reproduction, like the production of food and shelter, are basic forms of 'economic' or material necessity in any society. Only with the emergence of capitalism has 'economic' production come to be understood as a 'human' realm outside of 'nature'. Before capitalism, material production was understood, like sexuality and reproduction, to be 'natural' – precisely what human beings shared with animals. From the viewpoint of the dominant culture in previous societies what distinguished humanity was not production but rather culture, religion, politics, or some other 'higher' ideal made possible by the surplus appropriated from material production. In ancient Greece, for example, the labour of women and slaves within the household provided the material basis upon which male citizens could participate in the 'free' and 'democratic' world of the polis. Politics distinguished human life from the animal existence of women and slaves. Similarly, in medieval Europe, the surplus appropriated from peasant families supported the religious and aristocratic orders who together defined the purpose and meaning of the entire society. The serfs toiling in the field were understood as animals; they became human because they had 'souls' – i.e., they participated in religion. Before capitalism the family was associated with the 'natural' processes of eating, sleeping, sexuality, and cleaning oneself, with the agonies of birth, sickness, and death, *and* with the unremitting necessity of toil. It is this association of the family with the most primary and impelling material processes that has given it its connotation of backwardness as society advanced. Historically, the family has appeared to be in conflict with culture, freedom, and everything that raises humanity above the level of animal life. Certainly it is the association of women with this realm that has been among the earliest and most persistent sources of male supremacy and of the hatred of women.*

Capitalism, in its early development, distinguished itself from previous societies by the high moral and spiritual value it placed upon labour spent in goods production. This new esteem for production, embodied in the idea of private property and in the Protestant idea of a 'calling', led the early bourgeoisie to place a high value upon the family since the family was the basic unit of production. While in feudal society the 'personal' relations of the aristocracy were often highly self-conscious and carefully regulated, the domestic life of the masses was private and unexamined, even by the church. Early capitalism developed a high degree of consciousness concerning the internal life of the family and a rather elaborate set of rules and expectations that governed family life. This led to a simultaneous advance and retrogression in the status of women. On one hand, women were fixed more firmly than ever within the family unit; on the other hand, the family had a higher status than ever before. But the feminist idea that women in the family were outside the economy did not yet have any basis. As in pre-capitalist society, throughout most of capitalist history the family has been the basic unit of 'economic' production – not the 'wage-earning' father but the household as a whole. While

---

* H.R.Hays, in *The Dangerous Sex: The Myth of Feminine Evil*, New York 1972, gives a historical overview of male supremacy that indicates not only its persistence but the recurrence of identical themes. Almost, but not quite, universally, women are portrayed as dirty, bad-smelling, unhealthy, unspiritual, driven by sensuality and instinctual needs, weak, unreasoning and, in general, under the sway of brute necessity. Early myths such as those of Eve and Pandora also link women with both sexuality and the necessity of labour.

there was an intense division of labour *within* the family, based upon age, sex, and family position, there was scarcely a division *between* the family and the world of commodity production, at least not until the nineteenth century. Certainly women were excluded from the few 'public' activities that existed – for example, military affairs. But their sense of themselves as 'outside' the larger society was fundamentally limited by the fact that 'society' was overwhelmingly composed of family units based upon widely dispersed, individually owned productive property. Similarly, women had a respected role within the family since the domestic labour of the household was so clearly integral to the productive activity of the family as a whole.

But the overall tendency of capitalist development has been to socialize the basic processes of commodity production – to remove labour from the private efforts of individual families or villages and to centralize it in large-scale corporate units. Capitalism is the first society in history to socialize production on a large scale. With the rise of industry, capitalism 'split' material production between its socialized forms (the sphere of commodity production) and the private labour performed predominantly by women within the home. In this form male supremacy, which long antedated capitalism, became an institutional part of the capitalist system of production.

This 'split' between the socialized labour of the capitalist enterprise and the private labour of women in the home is closely related to a second 'split' – between our 'personal' lives and our place within the social division of labour. So long as the family was a productive unit based upon private property, its members understood their domestic life and 'personal' relations to be rooted in their mutual labour. Since the rise of industry, however, proletarianization separated most people (or families) from the ownership of productive property. As a result 'work' and 'life' were separated; proletarianization split off the outer world of alienated labour from an inner world of personal feeling. Just as capitalist development gave rise to the idea of the family as a separate realm from the economy, so it created a 'separate' sphere of personal life, seemingly divorced from the mode of production.

This development was a major social advance. It is the result of the socialization of production achieved by capitalism and the consequent decline in socially necessary labour time and rise in time spent outside production. Personal relations and self-cultivation have always, throughout history, been restricted to the leisure classes and to artists, courtiers, and others who performed the rituals of conversation, sexual encounter, self-examination, and physical and mental development according to well-developed and socially shared codes of behaviour. But under capitalism an ethic of personal fulfilment has become the property of the masses of people, though it has very different meanings for men and for women, and for different strata of the proletariat. Much of this search for personal meaning takes place within the family and is one reason for the persistence of the family in spite of the decline of many of its earlier functions.

The distinguishing characteristic of this search is its subjectivity – the sense of an individual, alone, outside society with no firm sense of his or her own place in a rationally ordered scheme. It takes place on a vast new social terrain known as 'personal' life, whose connection to the rest of society is as veiled and obscure as is the family's connection. While in the nineteenth century the family was still being studied through such disciplines as political economy and ethics, in the twentieth century it spawned its own 'sciences', most notably psychoanalysis and psychology. But psychology and psychoanalysis distort our understanding of personal life by assuming that it is governed by its own internal laws (for example, the psychosexual dynamics of the family, the 'laws' of the mind or of 'interpersonal relations') rather than by the 'laws' that govern society as a whole. And they encourage the idea that emotional life is formed only through the family and that the search for happiness should be limited to our 'personal' relations, outside our 'job' or 'role' within the division of labour.

Thus, the dichotomies that women's liberation first confronted – between the 'personal' and the 'political', and between the 'family' and the 'economy' – are rooted in the structure of capitalist society. All three writers reflect this split, as all three seek to overcome it. The means of overcoming it is through a conception of the family as a historically formed part of the mode of production.

The rise of capitalism isolated the family from socialized production as it created a historically new sphere of personal life among the masses of people. The family now became the major space in society in which the individual self could be valued 'for itself'. This process, the 'private' accompaniment of industrial development, cut women off from men in a drastic way and gave a new meaning to male supremacy. While housewives and mothers continued their traditional tasks of production – housework, child-rearing, etc. – their labour was devalued through its isolation from the socialized production of surplus value. In addition, housewives and mothers were given new responsibility for maintaining the emotional and psychological realm of personal relations. For women within the family 'work' and 'life' were not separated but were collapsed into one another. The combination of these forms of labour has created the specific character of women's labour within the family in modern capitalist society.

The following discussion is an attempt to understand the recent history of the family as part of the history of the capitalist mode of production. It describes two related historical transformations: the elimination of private productive property as the basis of the family among the masses of people, and the emergence of a sphere of personal life seemingly independent of the 'economy' and of 'production'.

Historians of the family in Europe and the United States have focused on its internal institutions – the laws of marriage, inheritance and divorce, the social relations of age and sex. Their emphasis has been formal and legalistic. Their major theories have stressed the slow, almost imperceptible evolution in the internal constitution of the household from the 'extended' to the 'nuclear' family. Viewed in this way, the seeming inertia of the family has been in marked contrast to the continuous upheaval of political and economic history, a contrast that lends plausibility to the view that 'history' is the realm of politics and economics while the family is confined to 'nature'.

In contrast, I have tried to understand the family as an integral part of a society that changes continuously and as a whole. I have focused on the continually changing social basis of the family as part of the organization of production. Under feudalism, kinship ties were of extreme importance, but the basic economic unit was the manor or the village economy. With the beginnings of capitalism, the bourgeoisie, in defending private productive property against feudal ties and restrictions, put forth a new conception of the family as an independent economic unit within a market economy. The bourgeois conception of private productive property underlies the 'discovery' of the family in the early modern period, the phenomenon described by Philippe Ariès in *Centuries of Childhood*.[14] Based upon private productive property, the ideology of the family as an 'independent' or 'private' institution is the counterpart to the idea of the 'economy' as a separate realm, one that capitalism over centuries wrested 'free' of feudal restrictions, customary law, and state and clerical intervention. Protestantism reinforced this conception of the family by making it a centre of religious observance.

In the early stages of industrial capitalism the family remained the productive unit, either through the 'putting out' system or by bringing the whole family into the early manufacturing institutions. But by the nineteenth century the factory system had eliminated many of the production functions of the family. The bourgeois family was reduced to the preservation and transmission of capitalist property, while the productive function of the proletarian family lay in the reproduction of the labour force. Hence, through the family each class reproduced its own class function. How did the proletarian family understand itself once it was stripped of private productive property?

To answer this question I have tried to describe the expansion of personal life among the masses of people in the nineteenth and twentieth centuries. Some of the origins of this process lie in the history of the family. The development of the bourgeois family encouraged individualism, self-consciousness and a new attention to domestic relations. But bourgeois individualism is inseparably linked to private productive property and economic competition. With the rise of industry, individualism begins to turn against capitalism itself in such movements as romanticism and utopian socialism. But these movements remained petty bourgeois insofar as they were based upon an obsolete ideal of private property. They proclaimed the unity of 'personal' and productive life in the form of self-contained cooperative economic units closely resembling the early bourgeois family.

By the twentieth century, a sphere of 'personal' life emerged among the proletariat itself. In the absence of a political movement that sought to transform both personal life and production, personal life was characterized by subjectivity – the search for personal identity outside the social division of labour. Having no private property to uphold, contemporary individualism upholds the self as an 'autonomous' realm outside society. This new emphasis on one's personal feelings and inner needs, one's 'head' or 'life style', to use contemporary formulations, gives a continued meaning to family life and at the same time threatens to blow it apart.

If we can understand the family as part of the development of capitalism this can help establish the specific historical formation of male supremacy. This, in turn, would help focus the attack upon it. The establishment of private productive property as the basis of the bourgeois household meant that society was organized into separate households each of which was ruled by the father (or grandfather). In the democratic proclamations of the bourgeois revolutions every defence of natural rights or individual freedom assumes that the (male) head of the household represents the women, children, and servants within. Similarly, women are invisible in the bourgeois exaltation of 'private property' or the 'yeoman'; the real 'yeoman' is the collective labour of the household. The emergence of personal life encouraged a sense of self-assertion and individual uniqueness among men while assigning women to the newly discovered worlds of childhood, emotional sensibility, and compassion, all contained within women's 'sphere', the family.

Personal life appears to take place in some private, psychological realm outside society. By its critique of male supremacy and of the family women's liberation has demonstrated its systematic and social character. The social terrain of personal life is the contemporary family within which men and women share so much, and in which their antagonism is so deeply rooted. The family is an important material basis for subjectivity in this society, and for psychological life generally. If we can simultaneously view it as part of the 'economy' a step would be taken toward understanding the connection between our inner emotional lives and capitalist development.

3.
Capitalism and the Family

An overall tendency toward dissolution has characterized formal kinship relations in Europe and the United States
in modern times. In feudal society kinship was integral to the
system of vassalage. The ruling aristocracy was organized as
a series of 'houses' or families, and pre-feudal clan and tribal
survivals underlay the village economy of the peasants.
Against the aristocratic emphasis on 'line' or 'blood', the
bourgeoisie asserted the right of every son to form his own
family. The bourgeois revolution represented the victory 'of
the family over the family name'. [15] With the rise of industrial
capitalism in the nineteenth and twentieth centuries the male-
dominated bourgeois family began to break up; the family
began to be reduced to its individual members, including
women and children. Each phase of dissolution has been
accompanied by a new attempt at synthesis – for the bourgeoisie the 'patriarchal' or 'nuclear' family, for the proletariat
'personal life'.

This chapter describes the place the family occupied in
the bourgeoisie's world outlook. Each succeeding ruling class
has incorporated and transformed the ideology of its predecessors. The rise of capitalism turned 'families' into units of commodity production. In the process, the bourgeoisie, through its
ideology of individualism based on private property, redefined
such feudal and pre-feudal ideals as male supremacy, family
loyalty, and romantic love. But the further development of
capitalism destroyed the basis of that ideology by turning

private property into capital and wage labour. When socialist, feminist, and other movements sought a new basis for family and personal life, they drew heavily on the bourgeois ideological heritage, often promising to realize the bourgeois ideal. For that reason I have focused on that heritage.

A note on the aristocracy

Family relations among the aristocracy were viewed and conducted as economic transactions. According to Christopher Hill, in seventeenth-century England 'the law of marriage . . . [was] almost the groundwork of the law of property'. [16] Marriage was arranged according to the family's rather than the individual's interest. Love and sexual life were sought outside marriage and mostly by men. Arranged marriages necessitated the double standard, mistresses, and illegitimacy. A major theme of the early bourgeoisie (one which was particularly clear in literature) was an attack on the cynical personal relations of the 'money power' and a defence of the family as the realm of *both* economic and personal life.

Aristocratic ideals of romantic love and individuality developed in explicit opposition to the family. In the refined society of the court, beyond the realm of goods production, the aristocracy developed an ideology of spiritualized but non-Christian love which prevailed only as adultery and which, in theory, was never consummated. Men, freed from the necessity of labour, were preoccupied with their personal relations and with an ideal of individual self-improvement.*

---

*Courtly love reflected the Catholic Church's distinction between sacred and secular love. Sacred love, like courtly love, existed outside the family and outside the realm of material production. Neither sacred nor courtly love was to be consummated. Similarly, the knightly quest for self-realization mimics the monastic stages of spiritual development, the emphasis on magic parallels the Catholic

Aristocratic women were exalted as spiritual creatures, as they later would be again, in the nineteenth century, when the bourgeois home lost its productive functions. In these respects and in its emphasis on the emotions, on sexuality and physical well-being, and on the free choice of a unique beloved, courtly love anticipated ideals of love and individualism that the bourgeoisie located within the family and that were generalized and transformed in the course of capitalist development.

The early bourgeois family in England

The prevalent form of family life in England before the rise of industry in the eighteenth and nineteenth centuries was that of an economically independent, commodity-producing unit. Often referred to as the 'patriarchal' family, it survives today only among the petty bourgeoisie. It originated between the disintegration of feudalism in the fourteenth century and the rise of capitalism in the sixteenth. During this period peasant families extricated themselves from feudal ties to become tenants or (far less often) landowners. In feudal society separate households were a subordinate part of a larger enterprise, generally the manor. While peasant families often worked as a unit, they had no independent economic initiative. Their holdings were in the form of narrow strips scattered amid those of other peasants 'in unfenced or open fields'.* The peasants shared the fields for cattle grazing; the harvest was gathered collectively. With the

---

ritual, the love of the lady parallels Mariolatry, and baptism is secularized in the rebirth of the knight. Heer points out that courtly love anticipates a long tradition of 'self-discovery' culminating in psychoanalysis. Frederick Heer, *The Medieval World*, New York 1962, pp.165–188.

*Barrington Moore Jr., *Social Origins of Dictatorship and Democracy*, Boston 1966, p.12.

decline of feudalism and the commercialization of agriculture some peasants were driven from the land while the holdings of others were consolidated as independent commodity-producing farms. Slowly, the family replaced the manor as the lowest social unit the head of which was an 'active citizen', able to buy and sell in the marketplace.[17]

On the basis of small-scale commodity production a new form of the family developed in the early bourgeois period. The household of a property-owning family in seventeenth-century England was a complicated economic enterprise that included not only children and relatives but servants, apprentices, and journeymen from different social classes. At its head was the *paterfamilias* who worked alongside his wife, children, employees, and wards. He was solely responsible for the economic and spiritual welfare of his family and represented in his person the supposed unity and independence of the family. The domestic relations of the household were an explicit part of the production relations of early capitalism.*

This bourgeoisie that emerged in England during the sixteenth and seventeenth centuries had many sources, including the landed nobility and the merchant capitalists of the medieval towns. But its most revolutionary sectors came from the class of small producers working their own property. For centuries the bourgeoisie identified itself with this form of production, distinguishing the 'industrious sort of people' from both the idle aristocracy and the shiftless poor. While family life differed vastly among different strata and classes, the early bourgeois family – the family as a self-contained productive unit –

---

* Only the *paterfamilias* could wear a hat in his own house. Christopher Hill points out that the *paterfamilias's* responsibility for the household foreshadows the paternalism that becomes so incongruous in the impersonal setting of developed capitalism. Hill, *Society and Puritanism*, pp. 449, 453.

furnished the basis for a new ideology of the family linked with the newly emerging ideas of private property and individualism. Much of this ideology was expressed through religion, particularly Puritanism, which was an inseparable part of the early bourgeois outlook. Taken together, the changes achieved by the bourgeoisie in seventeenth-century England established a new form of the family and an ethic of family life integral to the bourgeois system of rule.

The bourgeoisie encouraged a new respect for labour and economic activity. John Locke, writing toward the end of the century, expressed the bourgeois contempt for medieval 'other-worldliness':

> We are not born in heaven but in this world, where our being is to be preserved with meat, drink, and clothing, and other necessaries that are not born with us, but must be got and kept with forecast, care and labour, and therefore we cannot be all devotion, all praises and hallelujahs, and perpetually in the vision of things above.[18]

Locke expressed the view that through labour the individual expressed his own nature: 'Whatsoever [a man] removes out of the state that nature hath provided and left it in, he hath mixed his labour with, and joined to it something that is his own, and thereby makes it his property'.[19] This new value placed upon private property and productive labour encouraged a new esteem for the family.

The bourgeoisie's acceptance of economic life helped encourage a new acceptance of sexuality, eating, and other non-economic material processes of the family. The family had been scorned in medieval society as the realm of both production and sexuality. The Catholic Church, anti-sexual and savagely anti-female, had sanctioned family life only reluctantly, as the alternative to damnation, and had forbidden it to the clergy. The right of the clergy to marry had been a basic issue during the Reformation. In seventeenth-century England, Puritanism, with its acceptance of the life of material necessity, embraced the married state and exalted the family as part of the natural (i.e., God-given) order of productive and spiritual activity. Sexuality and emotional expression were encouraged, so long as they occurred within marriage. The Puritans condemned only 'unnatural' forms of sexuality such as the profligacy practiced at the court, and homosexuality, which they viewed with particular horror.[20] They argued that emotional and sexual expression must be 'weaned' – held within the bounds of nature and not carried to artificial excess. In *Paradise Lost*, a Puritan paean to the married state, Milton wrote, 'In loving thou dost well in passion not'.*

In contrast to the pre-capitalist divorce of spiritual and economic life, human meaning and purpose was now to be sought in the mundane world of production and the family. Throughout the Reformation, an ever-increasing proportion of religious instruction and prayer was removed from the church to the home. More important, Protestantism blessed the material labour performed by the family as sacred. Calvin answered the medieval text, 'Sell all thou hast and give to the poor', by saying, 'God sets more value on the pious management of a household'.[21] The family's economic life was now spiritualized. The Protestant idea of a 'calling' allowed one to do God's work in a secular craft or occupation.†

---

* Similarly Puritanism upheld the economically 'independent' individual (i.e., family) who held his own in the community, but attacked the 'unnatural' spirit of acquisitiveness associated with the rise of commerce.

† In Europe at this time the Catholic Church began to recognize the possibility of awarding sainthood to individuals in pursuits outside the clergy. The church began to encourage the laity in activities such as education previously monopolized by the clergy. Ariès, p. 357.

Underlying these changes was a new conception of human nature, that of possessive individualism. The bourgeoisie condemned the fixed stratification of medieval society as 'artificial' and viewed competitiveness based upon economic self-interest as the natural basis of society.* As market relations developed, the identification of the individual with a fixed social position began to give way to a commitment to the 'individual' (i.e., the individual family) who would rise or fall on the basis of independent efforts. The family came to be seen as a competitive economic unit apart from, and later even opposed to, the rest of society. In the seventeenth century competitiveness and acquisitiveness were still restricted by the corporate ideals of mercantilism, but by the eighteenth century they were generally encouraged.

The bourgeois acceptance of a certain degree of selfishness and aggression as part of human nature gave rise to a search for new principles of social order. While it was the vehicle of private ambition, the family was hierarchically organized and strictly disciplined. It forced the 'natural' materialism of its members to take a socially acceptable form. The early bourgeoisie understood the family to be the basic unit of the social order – 'a little church, a little state' – and the lowest rung in the ladder of social authority. They conceived of society as composed not of individuals but of families, each an indissoluble cell. If they spoke of 'indi-

---

*Shakespeare's plays, for example, defend the new early bourgeois ideals of love, marriage, and individual freedom on the basis of their being 'natural', i.e., outside convention. In *King Lear*, the established loyalties of the social order are posed against the individualism of the daughters, who wish to break away and live their own lives. The supremely egotistical figure in *Lear* is Edmund, who is a bastard, a child of 'nature', not part of society at all. Cf. Hill, *Society and Puritanism*, pp. 462–63.

42

vidual rights', it was because of the sovereignty of paternal power.

The new social and religious functions of the family led to a deepening consciousness concerning domestic life and to public debate over its form. Among Puritans and other sects it also led to a deepening *self*-consciousness, an awareness of one's internal psychological life. Christianity has always encouraged a certain degree of self-consciousness in the form of the conscience, the major form of subjective experience in Europe and America until the nineteenth century. But Puritans, and other Protestants, viewed social behaviour as a sign of inward grace and argued that no church ritual or other outward act could determine for certain whether an individual was 'saved'. One indication of the expansion of self-consciousness was the proliferation of diaries in the seventeenth century. More broadly, the same period saw the invention of silvered mirrors, the spread of autobiography, the building of chairs instead of benches, the spread of private lodgings, and the rise of self- portraits. In this period sincerity became a dominant social ideal.[22]

Taken together, these developments shaped a new ideal of family life. Marriage was coming to be understood as a partnership based upon common love and labour; one's wife was a companion or 'helpmeet'. The early bourgeois family gave rise to a new set of expectations based upon the couple's common destiny – not only love but mutual affection and respect, trust, fidelity, and pre-marital chastity. As in medieval society, children were quickly integrated into the adult order, but it was understood that when grown they would marry according to their own desires, although listening to their parents' counsel. In keeping with the high value placed upon both productive labour to expand the family's fortune and the weaning of one's emotions over time, maturity and old age were idealized. The symbol of the wise and self-disciplined grandfather now replaced, for a time, the more traditional image of the dotard.[23]

The bourgeois familial ideal obscured two contradictions that emerged in the course of capitalist development: the oppression of women and the family's subordination to class relations. The rise of the bourgeoisie entailed a simultaneous advance and retrogression in the position of women. In the economic life of medieval England women were closer to equality with men than they later were under capitalism. For example, women participated as equals in many guilds in the fourteenth century.[24] With the rise of capitalism they were excluded and, in general, economic opportunities for women not in families – such as spinsters or widows – declined. On the other hand women were given a much higher status within the family. For the Puritans, women's domestic labour was a 'calling', a special vocation comparable to the crafts or trades of their husbands. Like their husbands, women did God's work. As the lesser partner in a common enterprise, a woman was to be treated with respect. According to Robert Cleaver's *A Godly Form of Household Government*, a 1598 Puritan marriage manual, 'She was like a judge joined in commission to help rule his household. She was not to be made into a drudge or ordered about like a servant, but the husband was to command her "as the soul doth the body"',[25] i.e., through their mutual harmony. Wife-beating was now forbidden. And the Protestant conviction that all believers were spiritually equal rescued women from their medieval limbo of carnality. As in medieval peasant society, women were associated with the 'natural' realm of labour, but in contrast to medieval society this realm was highly valued.

Hence, women were encouraged to think of themselves

almost as independent persons at the same time that they were increasingly confined within the family. During the English Revolution the question of female equality was debated politically for the first time. Within many sects women played leading roles as preachers and organizers. (This was particularly true in sects that downgraded the importance of learning for salvation, since women were so little educated.)* These stirrings of women's equality reached a level in the seventeenth century sufficient to call forth a counter-movement among preachers and others that stressed female subordination within the family. One argument made was that the family was the economic property of the husband, and that married women owned nothing in their own right.[26]

So long as the family was considered the 'natural' or God-given basis of society, the issue of women's equality could not emerge on a large scale. The bourgeois view that the family (rather than individuals or classes) was the basic unit of society reinforced the deeply rooted traditions of male supremacy. And this view persisted as long as the family was a basic unit of social production. The issue of women's equality was largely muted until the late eighteenth and nineteenth centuries when the rise of industry finally destroyed the bourgeois ideal of the family as an independent productive unit.

That ideal had always been ideological, obscuring the class differences among the supposedly 'independent' producers of seventeenth-century England. According to the bourgeoisie, 'private property' established the family as an independent unit, guaranteed its political freedoms, and provided a new justification for the rule of the father. By 'private

---

* Episcopal documents of the period describe the sects as 'chiefly women', 'most silly women', and so forth. Keith Thomas, 'Women and the Civil War Sects', in Trevor Aston, *Crisis in Europe, 1560–1660*, New York 1967.

property' the seventeenth-century bourgeoisie meant both one's own labour power (i.e., 'property in one's person'), and the land or tools one employed. This obscured the fact that labour alone could never make one an 'independent' producer: farmers required land, implements, and stock; weavers required materials and the use of a loom.[27] Hence as capitalism developed, 'private property' divided – into capital on one hand, and labour power on the other.

In the seventeenth and eighteenth centuries this division took the form of 'domestic industry' – the family worked as a unit but in direct dependence on the capitalist class. Weavers, for example, were dependent upon merchant clothiers who supplied their wool, monopolized new technical inventions such as the knitting frame, finished the production of cloth by hiring workers, and served as intermediaries between the weaving family and the shopkeepers who sold their cloth. Only the ownership of land bestowed a measure of independence upon the artisan family.[28]

Domestic industry preserved the 'unity' but not the 'independence' of the original bourgeois ideal. E.P. Thompson somewhat romantically describes the family of weavers:

> The young children winding bobbins, older children watching for faults, picking over the cloth, or helping to throw the shuttle in the broad-loom; adolescents working a second or third loom; the wife taking a turn at weaving, in and among her domestic employments. The family was together, and however poor meals were, at least they could sit down at chosen times. A whole pattern of community life had grown up around the loom-shops; work did not prevent conversation or singing.[29]

Even the early forms of factory organization often preserved this unity. In the mills and manufacturing workshops of the early eighteenth century families worked as

46

a unit. Family and community relations were part of the hybrid organization of production in these early enterprises. For this reason, the early working class defended child labour, since it preserved the traditional ties between children and their parents (especially fathers, who transmitted a productive skill).[30]

Decline of the bourgeois family

The rise of the factory system made manifest the subjection of the family to the class relations of its members. Until then, the bourgeoisie had accommodated itself to domestic industry, since this was the most expedient and profitable way of organizing production. Once families were brought together in a common workshop, however, they were no longer supervised by the father but by the master. They no longer worked at their own rhythm, but according to the systematic labour discipline required by a coordinated division of labour. The master-manufacturer of the eighteenth century was obsessed with the necessity of instructing the workers in '"methodical" habits, punctilious attention to instructions, fulfilment of contracts to time, and in the sinfulness of embezzling materials.' In this context Methodism became the dominant religion of both bourgeoisie and working class. Unlike Puritanism, which asserted the unity of economic and spiritual life, Methodists preached the rigid division between the repression, discipline, and social subordination of daily life and the ritualized paroxysms of Sabbath emotionalism.[31]

The introduction of machinery was the culmination of this process, requiring human beings to 'identify themselves with the unvarying regularity of the complex automaton'.[32] Industrial capitalism required a rationalized, coordinated and synchronized labour process undisturbed by community sentiment, family responsibilities, personal relations or feelings. These changes in the organization of production led to the formation of a new ideology of the family. Earlier the bourgeoisie had portrayed the family as the progressive centre of individualism, but as industrial production destroyed the basis of the early bourgeois family, the family came to be either scorned as a backward institution or nostalgically romanticized. In either case it was contrasted to 'society', the system of social production and administration.

Jean-Jacques Rousseau, an early exponent of this contrast, identified the family with 'nature'. Like the early bourgeoisie, Rousseau idealized the family based upon private property. But unlike them he contrasted the 'spontaneously' developed, even 'primeval', division of labour within the family, to 'society'.[33] 'Society', he asserted, creates inequality, but 'nature' is inherently egalitarian: 'Neither master nor slave belongs to a family, but only to a class'.[34] 'Society' constricts human understanding within the narrow confines of rationality, which Rousseau calls 'philosophy', but within the family emotional life abounds, particularly compassion. 'It is philosophy that isolates a man; it is through philosophy that a man will secretly say, on seeing a man suffer: Die if you will, I am safe.' In the family the 'natural' sense of human solidarity still prevails, while in society it has been destroyed by the calculating egotism of the bourgeoisie. The early bourgeois family had been a microcosm of social authority. For Rousseau the family is held together 'voluntarily'* or through

---

* *Social Contract*, New York 1971, p. 8. Locke shared this idea. Both used it to combat defences of monarchical right that were based upon paternal authority within the family such as those by Filmer and Jean Bodin. Cf. Locke, *An Essay Concerning the True Original Extent and End of Civil Government*, part 6, 'Of Paternal Power'.

the 'natural' bonds of male supremacy.* In this regard he anticipates the modern belief in the internal freedom of the family and its determination by the emotional needs of its members. In contrast to the emotional life of the family, society was a rationalized programmed mechanism. One of the happiest moments of Rousseau's life came when, upon leaving Paris, he threw away his watch.[35] The family, attuned to the 'natural' rhythms of eating, sleeping, and child care, can never be wholly synchronized with the mechanized tempo of industrial capitalism.[36]

Rousseau's exaltation of domesticity was a late expression of the egalitarianism rooted in the bourgeois ideal of private property, as well as an early prefiguring of the romantic and utopian socialist critique of capitalism. Rousseau's 'family' is the petty bourgeois household, part of a society of 'independent producers'. But the bourgeois family was losing its earlier productive role. Even the most basic domestic tasks, such as child-rearing, were being performed by servants. And as production became increasingly socialized, the bourgeoisie lost its illusion of individual autonomy within the sphere of goods production. By the nineteenth century the bourgeoisie had formulated a very different ideal of the family – that of an enclave protected from industrial society. Although this ideal was based upon the *bourgeois* family it also pervaded petty bourgeois and proletarian family life and shaped the movements to transform the family that arose in the nineteenth century.

In the early nineteenth century, the bourgeoisie saw

---

*Though Rousseau already reflects the division of labour between the sexes based upon wage-labour: 'Woman, honour your master, he it is who works for you, he it is who gives you bread to eat; this is he!' *Emile*, p. 401.

themselves as alienated from both 'society' – the Franken-stein monster they had created – and 'nature' – the world they had left behind. Reflecting the brutal, seemingly irresist-ible, imposition of industrial capitalism, 'society' was en-visioned as a vast economic machine.

The idea of self-interest now supplanted the idea of conscience and money came to dominate all social relations. According to Jeremy Bentham: 'The preparation in the human bosom for antipathy towards other men is, under all circumstances, most unhappily copious and active.' The reason?

> The boundless range of human desires, and the very limited number of objects . . . Human beings are the most powerful instruments of production, and therefore everyone becomes anxious to employ the services of his fellows in multiplying his own comforts.

According to Bentham it was futile to 'dive into the unfathomable regions of motives' since all that was necessary was to know what one wanted. Indeed, man is 'by interest diverted from any close examination into the springs by which his own conduct is determined. From such knowledge he has not, in any ordinary shape, anything to gain – he finds not in it any source of enjoyment.' In this species of economic determinism men and women would know each other 'solely from the outside' and through a busy life of getting and spending would avoid what Bentham called the 'painful probe' of introspection.[37]

Because of the need to recycle all wealth into the process of capital accumulation, the nineteenth-century bourgeoisie put forth an ethic of self-abnegation and denial.[38] 'Capital', wrote the political economist N.W.Senior, is 'abstinence'. According to John Stuart Mill, 'everything that is produced perishes and most things very quickly . . . Capital is kept in existence from age to age not by preservation, but by perpetual reproduction'. 'We economize with our health, our capacity for enjoyment, our forces', wrote Sigmund Freud in 1883, 'we save up for something, not knowing ourselves for what'.[39] Nature now appeared cruel and alien. Malthus's theory of population summed up the nineteenth-century belief that nature, in some sort of vicious joke, had instilled men and women with a sexual instinct that led them to produce offspring while simultaneously limiting the potential subsistence it would supply. In this context of scarcity, mutual suspicion, and a deep sense of the inner worthlessness of the world they had created, the Victorian bourgeoisie came to idealize the new, protected family, outside nature and outside production.

The family, to the Victorian bourgeoisie, was a 'tent pitch'd in a world not right'.[40] 'This is the true nature of home', wrote John Ruskin and,

> it is the place of peace; the shelter, not only from all injury, but from all terror, doubt, and division. . . . So far as the anxieties of the outer life penetrate into it . . . it ceases to be a home; it is then only a part of the outer world which you have roofed over and lighted fire in.[41]

It stood in opposition to the terrible anonymous world of commerce and industry: 'a world alien, not your world . . . without father, without child, without brother.'[42] The Victorian family was distinguished by its spiritual aspect: it is remote, ethereal and unreal – 'a sacred place, a vestal temple'.[43] As in the middle ages, so now with the bourgeoisie, the domain of the spirit had once again separated off from the realm of production.

Reflecting this separation, the belief in separate 'spheres' for men and women came to dominate the ideology of the family in the epoch of industrial capitalism. As the family was now idealized, so was the familial role of women.

According to one of the domestic manuals that began to flourish in the 1830s and 1840s, 'that fierce conflict of worldly interests, by which men are so deeply occupied, [compels them] to stifle their best feelings'.[44] Men, according to Ruskin, are 'feeble in sympathy'.[45] But women, by contrast, whose 'everyday duties are most divine because they are most human', nurture within the family the 'human' values crushed by 'modern life'.[46] Earlier, the feudal aristocracy had idealized women for their delicate beauty. In the eighteenth century the bourgeoisie had stressed their role as practical and intelligent housewives. Now the dominant image of women was that of the mother who, freed from domestic labour by the abundance of servants could devote herself wholly to her child.[47] 'A woman when she becomes a mother should withdraw herself from the world', instructed an 1869 domestic manual.[48] In the nineteenth century, childhood was first assigned a separate identity and exalted as the time of life untainted by the roughness of material necessity.* To a large extent sexual interest was removed from the bourgeois family and assigned to prostitutes, an important group among working-class women. Filial relations were intensified and charged with unsuspected emotions by the sexual repression and prudery characteristic of the period of capital accumulation. As Freud soon demonstrated, the Victorian bourgeois family was a cauldron of anger, jealousy, fear and guilt – not

---

* Describing a parallel transformation in American life, Ralph Waldo Emerson expressed the paradoxical quality of the nineteenth-century exaltation of childhood through the remark of a friend who recalled the hardships of his own youth: 'It was a misfortune to have been born when children were nothing and to live till men were nothing.' 'Historic Notes of Life and Letters in New England', in Perry Miller, ed., *The American Transcendentalists*, New York 1957, p. 5.

to mention sexuality. But its internal, subjective life was masked by the stark contrast between its protective warmth and the 'universal thirst for power'[49] that prevailed in society. Even men could find their 'true self' in the family, 'no longer stained by contact with the . . . petty spite and brutal tyranny of an office'.[50] This vision of the family was incorporated and systematized within the realm of moral philosophy. John Stuart Mill, for example, praised its 'loving forgetfulness of self'[51] and Hegel argued that it was the 'naturally ethical' antithesis to the brutal competition of civil society.[52]

Victorian idealism represented a decline from the early bourgeois conception of the family. Just as the bourgeoisie was being transformed into a parasitic class within the system of production, so its ideology of the family was becoming abstract and idealized. Within this decline the bourgeois family was called into question by the new social movements of the late eighteenth and nineteenth centuries.

Beginning in the eighteenth century a series of writers and artists attacked the bourgeois ideal of the family on behalf of free love. Drawing upon the arguments of William Godwin, Percy Shelley wrote, 'Love withers under constraint: its very essence is liberty: it is compatible neither with obedience, jealousy, nor fear.' Shelley urged the abolition of marriage, and expected that the result would be unions 'of long duration', marked by generosity and self-devotion, since 'choice and change will be exempted from restraint'.[53] In its origins, the support for free love was closely related to an attack on the social repression of women.

Feminism in England had two different sources. Among middle-class women it represented a protest against the enforced domesticity brought about by the rise of industry. The withdrawal of commodity production from the home radically separated women from men; the creation of a separate 'sphere' for women also laid the basis for a separate women's movement. Women attacked the genteel idleness of the 'doll's house' and demanded entry into education, the professions, and public life. Simultaneously, working-class women were being drawn into large-scale industry. Demands for female suffrage and related reforms were raised within the proletarian movement generally – for example, among the National Union of the Working Classes and the Chartists. Both groups of women often reconciled their demands with support for the traditional domestic values of the bourgeois household.

The Victorian opposition to female equality was bitter and furious, reflecting the idea that the family had become the last refuge from the demands of capitalist society. The emancipation of women threatened to degrade all society to a common level of cynical manipulation (i.e., economic competition in the marketplace). Within the same bourgeois view, feminists argued that bringing women into society would humanize it. Nineteenth-century feminism was closely involved with movements of moral reform such as temperance and the abolition of prostitution. Their participation in these movements supported the idea that women were the guardians of society's morals. Similarly, on the basis of their special capacity for service, certain occupations, for example schoolteaching and nursing, were largely restricted to women, and downgraded.

To the feminist attack on the Victorian ideal the socialists' voice was added. The rise of industrial capitalism had created a new form of the family among the bourgeoisie, but it had eliminated the economic basis of the family – private productive property – among the working class. As Engels wrote in his 1844 description of the English working class:

Family life for the worker is almost impossible under the existing social system . . . The various members of the family only see each other in the mornings and evenings, because the husband is away at his work all day long. Perhaps his wife and the older children also go out to work and they may be in different factories. In these circumstances how can family life exist?[54]

Marx and Engels rejected the nineteenth-century idealization of the bourgeois family, which they viewed as the retrograde preserve of private wealth. In contrast to Hegel and Mill they insisted that 'civil society' or 'political economy' – capitalism – directly infected family life. 'On what foundation is the present family, the bourgeois family, based?' they wrote in the *Communist Manifesto*. 'On capital. On private gain . . . The bourgeois sees in his wife a mere instrument of production' whereas, among the proletariat, 'all family ties . . . are torn asunder'. According to Marx and Engels the early bourgeois ideals of the family – love, equality, and common work – could not be realized so long as society was organized around private property. The family under capitalism, ostensibly private, was in fact continually transformed by the needs of the dominant class. Communism would liberate the family from its subjection to capital and 'will make the relations between the sexes a purely private affair, which concerns only the two persons involved'.[55] Hence in the nineteenth century a series of movements arose directed at 'private' or family life. The following chapter describes their social origins.

4.
Proletarianization and the Rise of Subjectivity

The transformation of bourgeois individualism

In feudal society men and women occupied a fixed position within a stratified division of labour – they owed allegiance to a particular lord and worked on a particular plot of land rather than being 'free' to sell their labour or property. Explicit and direct relations of authority defined people's sense of individual identity. Catholicism provided them with a common purpose outside themselves.

Private property freed the early bourgeoisie from a fixed social role within the feudal order. On the basis of private property the bourgeoisie has defended 'individual rights' throughout history – first against feudal prerogative, more recently against labour unions and 'state intervention'. The bourgeoisie has consistently defended the right of individuals to rise and fall within the marketplace through their own efforts, rather than on the basis of birth; the bourgeoisie originated the idea of a necessary contradiction between the individual and society.

But bourgeois individualism also serves as a basis for social order within capitalist society. Based upon private property, bourgeois individualism was identified with a particular activity – commodity production – and a predetermined inner life – the Christian conscience and self-interest. Major bourgeois social theories such as liberalism or rationalism posit a society of individuals (i.e., families) who, acting in their own self-interest, advance the social purpose by expanding private wealth: while individuals compete against one another, the marketplace guarantees a coherent social whole. Similarly, bourgeois moral ideals combine an emphasis on being true to oneself – direct, unashamed – with an emphasis on performing one's social obligations. In this view the property owner and his authoritarian family ('a little commonwealth') are the centre of a well-ordered society.

The development of large-scale industrial production destroyed this unity. In a process that lasted several centuries but that culminated in the nineteenth century in England and the United States, productive property was virtually monopolized by a small centralized ruling class. The centre of social authority shifted from the property-owning family to remote centres of power. The British radical Thomas Cobbett wrote in the early nineteenth century that industry had drawn 'the resources of the country unnaturally together into great heaps'.[56] Work, in the form of wage-labour, was removed from the centre of family life, to become the means by which family life was maintained. Society divided and the family became the realm of 'private life'.

At the same time the conflict between the individual and society took on a new meaning. On one side appeared 'society' – the capitalist economy, the state, the fixed social core that has no space in it for the individual; on the other, the personal identity, no longer defined by its place in the social division of labour. On one side the objective social world appeared, perceived at first as 'machinery' or 'industry', then throughout the nineteenth century as 'society' and into the twentieth as 'big business', 'city hall', and then as 'technology' or 'life', as the domination of the proletariat by the capitalist class became more difficult to perceive. In opposition to this harsh world that no individual could hope to affect, the modern world of subjectivity was created.

This sense of an isolated individual ranged against a society he or she cannot affect, distinguishes social life in developed capitalist society. The major tradition of modern bourgeois social thought, as exemplified in the work of Freud and Weber, portrays the conflict between the 'individual' and 'society' as the 'human condition' and thereby encourages 'mature' acquiescence to the demands of capital. But there is also a tradition of protest. Its earliest expression did not come from the proletariat but from the petty bourgeois and artisan classes who, as society divided between capital and wage labour, resisted proletarianization. Beginning in the late eighteenth and early nineteenth centuries petty bourgeois individualism perpetually ranged itself against the emerging bourgeoisie, and perpetually lost. But political and economic weakness was accompanied by ideological strength. Petty bourgeois individualism defended what was most progressive in the bourgeois past while articulating what was most oppressive in the condition of the emerging proletariat. It spoke for the whole individual before the deformations of the capitalist division of labour. It argued that one's work should be an expression of oneself rather than just a means to survival. Petty bourgeois individualism continually threatened to burst and overflow the private property integument that enclosed it and to envision the individual as an end in him or herself.

In the nineteenth century the romantic artist was the great symbol of the individual posed against society. Before the rise of industrial capitalism artists occupied a fixed place within an explicit division of labour. Writers lived on 'pensions, benefices and sinecures', composers were 'court musicians, church musicians or town musicians', painters were commissioned by patrons.[57] In this regard the production relations of artists were similar to those of other pre-industrial artisans whose income and position were based less on supply and demand than on custom, social prestige, and traditional standards of pay and workmanship.[58] By the early 1800s the artist was producing commodities for newly arisen industries: commercial publishing, popular periodicals, newspapers, galleries and commercial concerts. The artist's defence against proletarianization lay in a new emphasis on the originality of the artist and the uniqueness of the work of art. Beginning with romanticism, artists declared that art was the product less of a particular craft or discipline than of the artist's inner life. 'What information does a poet require?' asked Wordsworth in 1800; unlike 'a lawyer, a physician, a mariner, an astronomer, or a natural philosopher' only that which he possesses 'as a man' – 'the sympathies of our daily life'.[59] Wordsworth spoke for the artist, but it was the universality of the experience of pitting oneself, one's inner feelings, private thoughts, and dreams, against 'society' that inspired the modern image of the artist.

Wordsworth looked back to 'humble and rustic life' in which 'the essential passions of the heart find a better soil'. But this ideal had lost its social basis with the rise of industrial capitalism. Throughout the nineteenth century the romantic tradition conjured up a series of figures who allegedly stood apart from society on the basis of their own personal uniqueness: the hero, the virtuoso, the mystic, the world traveller, the wandering Jew, the mountain climber; figures who constantly threaten to disappear from society.[60] The idea of the genius also comes from this period, as well as the idea of the dandy who turns his personal life into art. But dandyism, according to Charles Baudelaire, depends on people 'free from the need to follow any profession. They have no other purpose than to ... satisfy their desires, and to feel and think'.[61] Romantic individualism's final expression, in twentieth-century art, would confine the individual to an entirely subjective and psychological realm, wholly divorced from the rest of society.

The defence of the subjective individual against 'science', 'industry', or 'modern society' continued throughout the nineteenth century. Its characteristic tone was one of protest: for example, Thomas Carlyle in 1829: 'Not the external and physical alone is now managed by machinery but the internal and spiritual also . . . Men are grown mechanical.'[62] Against the general rationalization of life the romantic tradition upheld the view that men and women were feeling beings. It saw in 'nature' (which eventually came to include sexuality) 'the repository of [those] inner tendencies opposing the growth of mechanisation, dehumanisation and reification'.[63] In its emphasis on the emotions, on innocence and childhood, on love and on beauty, romanticism invoked a world in which human beings were no longer dominated by the daily discipline of production. In this way, a tradition deeply rooted in the bourgeois ideal of individualism also came to stand for a qualitatively different way of life.

The socialist movement, which arose in the nineteenth century, was closely linked to this romantic tradition, particularly through its utopian forebears. The concept of alienation derived from the same milieu as the artist's assertion that one's product is a part of oneself. Marx invoked a conception of human activity closely related to the romantic vision:

> The ancient conception in which man always appears (in however narrowly national, religious, or political a definition) as the aim of production, seems very much more exalted than the modern world in which production is the aim of man and wealth the aim of production. In fact, however, when the narrow bourgeois form has been peeled away, what is wealth, if not the universality of needs, capacities, enjoyments, productive powers, etc. of individuals, produced in universal exchange?[64]

60

On the other hand, socialism developed in the nineteenth century by defining itself off from this romantic and utopian tradition. Romanticism represented an ideological understanding of capitalist society, and throughout the nineteenth century aligned itself as easily with conservative and reactionary political currents as with socialism. Socialists downgraded the split it portrays between the 'individual' and 'society' as the expression of a declining class whose productive function was being eliminated. The romantic tradition exalted the 'lone individual' at a time when society was dividing irrevocably into two classes. And, indeed, it is likely that the romantic tradition of individualism would have dwindled into obscurity if the rise of capitalism had not created a new social basis for it in the proletarian family.

Proletarianization created a new form of the family among the masses of people – one 'separated' off from the sphere of goods production. Within it, new needs began to take shape. For those reduced to proletarian status from the petty bourgeoisie, one's individual identity could no longer be realized through work or through the ownership of property: individuals now began to develop the need to be valued 'for themselves'. Proletarianization gave rise to subjectivity. The family became the major sphere of society in which the individual could be foremost – it was the only space that proletarians 'owned'. Within it, a new sphere of social activity began to take shape: personal life. The nineteenth century Victorian ideology of the family as the repository of 'human values' converged with the tradition of romantic revolt. The proletariat itself came to share the bourgeois ideal of the family as a 'utopian retreat'. Although this development did not emerge clearly until the twentieth century, its preconditions were established in the early stages of industrial capitalism.

61

The proletarian family

With the rise of industrial capitalism wages replaced productive property as the economic basis of the family. 'Private property' was redefined among the proletariat to refer to objects of consumption: food, clothing, domestic articles, and later, for some, a home. The traditional division of labour within the family was threatened as women and children joined men in the factories. Meanwhile, capital was accumulated by restricting domestic consumption and diverting any surplus into industry. The bourgeois ethic of repression and abstinence was extended to the proletariat through the force of material circumstances. The family's internal life was dominated by the struggle of its members for their basic material needs.

This understanding underlay the politics of nineteenth-century socialists and reformers. Many feared that by turning women and children into wage-earners, industrial capitalism was destroying the family. The goal of 'saving' the family underlay such nineteenth-century reforms as protective legislation and child labour laws. Over time a series of private and public institutions arose – schools, savings banks, insurance companies, welfare agencies – whose function was to mediate between capitalist production and the fragmented realm of private life. The great trade union struggles through which the nineteenth-century working class both resisted and accommodated itself to industrial capitalism were also intended to establish a new basis for the proletarian family. Women were commonly excluded from trade unions and male trade unionists demanded a wage that could support the entire family.

When the socialist movement took up the question of the family in the nineteenth century it expected that a revolution in commodity production would simultaneously transform the family; early socialists did not experience the family as a 'separate' political problem. The major critique of the family came from within romantic and utopian socialist currents and from feminists. The great effect that Marx and Engels had on nineteenth-century socialism was to demonstrate the centrality of the sphere of commodity production (the sphere in which surplus value was produced and realized) to all areas of life. This gave the romantic and utopian critique a theoretical basis that it lacked, and encouraged a focus on collective political action rather than on individual transformation. But it also led away from the emphasis on subjective or personal life that distinguishes the petty bourgeois tradition. Reflecting the struggle for survival that characterized the nineteenth-century proletarian family, Marx and Engels saw no need for a separate programme for 'personal' life, including the oppression of women by men within the family. Instead they believed that if individuals were freed from economic exploitation they would arrange their private lives according to earlier ideals of domestic and personal fulfilment, unrealizable under conditions of industrial capitalism.

The development of capitalism destroyed this hope and to a great extent 'separated' the socialist movement from the subsequent development of the family and of personal life among the proletariat. The reduction of the economically 'independent' family to a houseworker and a factory worker was part of a process that led to greatly expanded productivity of labour. In the face of a growing labour movement, European and American capitalists began to meet some trade union demands, while diverting the working class from its attack against capitalist production.

By the middle of the nineteenth century bourgeois economists in England and America had begun to argue that the development of leisure time among the workers coupled with a rise in wages would benefit capital by greatly expanding the domestic market for consumer goods. This argument was also adopted by the labour movement. In 1863, for example, an American labour spokesman, Ira Steward, called for *A Reduction of Hours, An Increase of Wages* which jointly would encourage 'the workers, through their new leisure, to unite in buying luxuries now confined to the wealthy'.[65] In the second half of the nineteenth century the great industries of domestic consumption arose in England: clothing, food, furniture, housing.[66] By the end of the century bourgeois spokesmen were proclaiming that workers were becoming 'capitalists', since a frugal and fortunate working family could in some cases eventually purchase its own home. Along with this, the bourgeoisie encouraged the belief that human meaning could be found primarily within the sphere of consumption.

At the same time, women and children lost the central place they had occupied in the early proletariat. Child labour was slowly eliminated and women were transformed into a marginal labour force in relation to capitalist production, with their primary loyalty to the home. The housewife emerged, alongside the proletarian – the two characteristic labourers of developed capitalist society. Her tasks extended beyond the material labour of the family to include responsibility for the 'human values' which the family was thought to preserve: love, personal happiness, domestic felicity. In contrast, the working-class husband's primary responsibility was understood to be earning a wage, whether or not his wife worked. The split in society between 'personal feelings' and 'economic production' was integrated with the sexual division of labour. Women were identified with emotional life, men with the struggle for existence. Under these conditions a new form of the family developed – one that understood itself to be operating in apparent freedom from production, and that placed a primary emphasis on the personal relations of its members. A separate sphere of personal life began to develop among the proletariat. This development can be seen most clearly in the twentieth-century United States.

Personal life and subjectivity in the twentieth-century United States

As capitalism developed the productive functions performed by the family were gradually socialized.* The family lost its core identity as a productive unit based upon private property. Material production within the family – the work of housewives and mothers – was devalued since it was no longer seen as integral to the production of commodities. The expansion of education as well as welfare, social work, hospitals, old age homes, and other 'public' institutions further eroded the productive functions of the family. At the same time the family acquired new functions as the realm of personal life – as the primary institution in which the search for personal happiness, love, and fulfilment takes place. Reflecting the family's 'separation' from commodity production, this search was understood as a 'personal' matter, having little relation to the capitalist organization of society.

The development of this kind of personal life among the masses of people was a concomitant of the creation of a working class in capitalist society. Peasants and other pre-capitalist labourers were governed by the same social rela-

---

* Although much of the following also applies to black and other 'third world' families, there are also enormous differences that I do not discuss. A good starting place for such a discussion is Angela Davis, 'Reflections on the Black Woman's Role in the Community of Slaves', *Black Scholar*, December 1971.

tions 'inside' and 'outside' work; the proletarian, by contrast, was a 'free' man or woman outside work. By splitting society between 'work' and 'life', proletarianization created the conditions under which men and women looked to themselves, outside the division of labour, for meaning and purpose. Introspection intensified and deepened as people sought in themselves the only coherence, consistency, and unity capable of reconciling the fragmentation of social life. The romantic stress on the unique value of the individual began to converge with the actual conditions of proletarian life, and a new form of personal identity developed among men and women, who no longer defined themselves through their jobs. Proletarianization generated new needs – for trust, intimacy, and self-knowledge, for example – which intensified the weight of meaning attached to the personal relations of the family. The organization of production around alienated labour encouraged the creation of a separate sphere of life in which personal relations were pursued as an end in themselves.

But the creation of a separate sphere of personal life was also shaped by the special problems of the capitalist class in the early twentieth century. Increasing proletarianization, along with deepening economic crises, created increasing labour unrest and class conflict, as well as the growth of the socialist movement. Beginning in the early twentieth century a significant minority of American capitalists saw the possibility of integrating labour within a capitalist consensus through raising its level of consumption. Besides expanding the market for consumer goods, such a strategy would divert the working class from socialism and from a direct assault on capitalist relations of production. Edward Filene, for example, a Boston department store owner, urged his fellow capitalists to recognize unions and raise wages as a way of extending 'industrial democracy' and 'economic freedom' to the working class. 'The industrial democracy I am discussing', he explained, 'has nothing to do with the Cubist politics of class revolution'. Instead, he urged that workers be free to 'cultivate themselves' in the 'school of freedom' which the modern marketplace constituted. 'Modern workmen have learned their habits of consumption ... in the school of fatigue', but mass production was transforming the consumer market into a 'civilizing' experience for the working class.[67] The emphasis on consumption was an important means through which the newly proletarianized, and still resisting, industrial working class was reconciled to the rise of corporate capitalism, and through which the enormous immigrant influx of the late nineteenth and early twentieth centuries was integrated with the industrial working class.

The extraordinary increases in the productivity of labour achieved during the nineteenth century, along with increasing American dominance within the world market, made it possible for capitalists to pursue this course. By the 1920s many firms had acceded to the sustained demand for a shorter work-day. This demand, probably the most persistent trade union demand of the nineteenth century, was the necessary pre-requisite to the establishment of personal life among the proletariat: it freed life-time from the immediate demands of capital. In the nineteenth century, socialists had emphasized the eight-hour day, since it would free the working class for self-education and political activity. But with the decline of American socialism after World War I, this issue receded. In the 1930s the eight-hour day and the forty-hour week became the standard in mass-production industry. Work time has been fixed at these levels ever since, in spite of subsequent technological progress. The capitalist class has extended 'leisure' to the proletariat, but only within the limits set by the capitalists' need to retain control of the labour force.

Similarly, the capitalist class has raised wages in accord with its overall interests. Monopoly control of the market made it possible for capitalists to 'compensate' themselves for wage increases by simultaneously raising prices. Beginning in the 1930s state programmes such as welfare and unemployment insurance financed a minimum level of consumption among the entire working class by taxing its better-paid sectors. Along with these measures corporate capitalists created a sales force and employed the new media of radio and television to spread the ethic of consumerism into every home.

The family, no longer a commodity-producing unit, received a new importance as a market for industrial commodities. Mass production forced the capitalist class to cultivate and extend that market, just as it forced it to look abroad for other new markets. As a result, American domestic and personal life in the twentieth century has been governed by an ethic of pleasure and self-gratification previously unknown to a labouring class. Working people now see consumption as an end in itself, rather than as an adjunct to production, and as a primary source of both personal and social (i.e., 'status') identity. This is often expressed within the 'middle class' as 'lifestyle', a word that is used to defend one's prerogatives regardless of the demands of 'society'.

The rise of 'mass consumption' has vastly extended the range of 'personal' experience available to men and women while retaining it within an abstract and passive mode: the purchase and consumption of commodities. Taste, sensibility, and the pursuit of subjective experience – historically reserved for leisure classes and artists – have been generalized throughout the population in predetermined and standardized forms by advertising and other means. This is reflected in the modern department store in which the wealth, culture, and treasures of previous ruling classes now appear in the form of cheap jewellery, fashions, and housewares.*

On one hand there has been a profound democratization of the idea that it is good to live well, consume pleasurably, and enjoy the fruits of one's labour. On the other hand, 'mass consumption' – within the context of capitalism – has meant the routinization of experience and the deepening of divisions within the proletariat. The deep material deprivation that still characterizes the lives of most Americans – bitter inadequacies of housing, food, transportation, health care, etc. – has taken on added emotional meanings. The 'poor' feel personally inadequate and ashamed, while the more highly educated and better-paid sectors of the working class experience guilt toward the 'less fortunate'.

In developed capitalist society, the enhancement of personal consumption has been closely related to the devaluation of labour. Like the rise of mass consumption, the idea that labour is worthless results from its vastly expanded productivity. Expanded production of necessary goods – for example, food, clothing, and housing – without expanding the labour time spent in such production, began in agriculture

---

* Honoré de Balzac noted a similar phenomenon in the Paris arcades of the 1820s and 1830s, perhaps the earliest form of the department store: 'The magic columns of these palaces show to the connoisseur on every side in the articles which their portals display that *industry rivals the arts*'. Quoted in Walter Benjamin, 'Paris - Capital of the Nineteenth Century', *New Left Review*, March 1968, p. 77. Italics added

after the Civil War and in manufacturing during the 1920s.* As a result, the sphere of necessary goods production has shrunk in relation to other spheres of production. To counteract the effects of this tendency – particularly rising unemployment – and to maintain a level of 'scarcity' in consumer goods, corporate capitalism has fostered inflation, waste, planned obsolescence, and under-utilization of productive capacity. It has vastly expanded 'non-productive' industries such as advertising and finance, and used the state to subsidize the production of useless or destructive goods, such as armaments. A great amount of labour time in capitalist society is spent in activities that have the purpose of perpetuating capitalist relations of production, rather than producing necessary goods. This deepening irrationality of capitalist production has obscured the place of production within our society.

In the nineteenth century, every sacrifice to the engine of capital accumulation was justified in the name of 'material necessity', the driving force of all previous human history. Similarly, socialists defined their revolution in terms of taking over the productive capacity as it had been developed under capitalism. But in the twentieth century the centre no longer

---

* Martin J. Sklar, 'On the Proletarian Revolution and the End of Political-Economic Society', *Radical America*, May 1969, terms this tendency 'disaccumulation' to contrast it with the accumulation process of industrial capitalism. In some way every attempt to describe what has changed in capitalism since the nineteenth century must make this tendency central. For example, Paul Baran and Paul Sweezy's *Monopoly Capital*, New York 1966 refers to it as the tendency of the surplus to rise. Other examples include Maurice Dobb, 'Some Features of Capitalism since the First World War', in *Capitalism, Development and Planning*, New York 1970, pp. 38–39, and Tom Nairn and Angelo Quattrocchi, *The Beginning of the End*, London 1968, pp. 156–73.

holds. Most people see no meaning or value in their work. In addition, marginal employment and unemployment characterize major groups in American society – youth, housewives, 'hippies', the black 'lumpenproletariat'. Within these groups, which are themselves marginal to the sphere of commodity production, the idea has developed that production is itself marginal to social life.

This tendency has also been reinforced within the sphere of goods production. In the nineteenth century the capitalist class and its representatives directly supervised the labour process. By contrast, capitalists are often physically absent in the modern corporation. Instead the labour process appears to be governed by neutral, scientific laws such as centralization, efficiency, the imperatives of technology, etc. This appearance reflects the increasing rationalization of the labour process and reinforces the tendency to understand modern society in terms of the domination of the individual by anonymous, impersonal forces. Rather than encountering the capitalist class, the proletariat is faced by abstract, scientific laws and 'countless, immediate oppressors'.[68]

The combination of waste, under-employment, and rationalization has come close to destroying people's understanding of their part in an integrated system of social production. It has reinforced the tendency to look to personal life for meaning, and to understand personal life in entirely subjective terms. The isolation of so much of modern life from the sphere of necessary goods production gives it its 'abstract' character. Both 'society' and personal life are experienced as formless, with no common core, in inexplicable disarray.

The changing character of developed, capitalist production has expanded personal life in constricted, capitalist forms. As opportunities for capital investment have declined within the sphere of necessary goods production, capital has spread to the sphere of personal life. Whole new industries – the 'services' – have developed in this way.[69] Examples include the media and other forms of culture, travel, sports, psychotherapy, health, and commercial religions. Since production no longer integrates social life, the capitalist class has sought new means of social solidarity. In particular the education system has been assigned the function of teaching people to 'get along' with one another.[70] The increasing role of mental labour within the process of production has entailed the creation of new skills such as 'imagination' and 'sensitivity', which have in turn shaped personal life.

Both the emphasis on salesmanship, integral to the rise of mass production, and the emphasis of the services and the state on 'working with people' have encouraged an attention to psychology and new forms of sensitivity. Insight into the personal lives of others, gained to a large extent through self-awareness, has been taught to large sectors of the working class: it has become a productive skill necessary to capitalist development. Similarly the working class and petty bourgeoisie have been urged to shed the 'selfish individualism' associated with laissez-faire capitalism, in favour of co-operation, sociability, and tolerance.* But 'cooperation' and 'sociability' are enforced through authoritarian institutions such as the public schools that have the responsibility – and power – to make people get along with one another.

Similarly, the increasingly technological character of modern production has created a need for workers with abilities of self-expression, independence, and creativity. But the

---

* This ideal ['the family of man'], like the ideals generated by mass consumption, takes the form of a conflict between the 'new middle class' and the rest of the proletariat.

educational system has cloaked these skills in an ideology of personal development rather than presenting them as necessary skills of production. As a result men and women (but particularly men) have been encouraged to dwell upon their own uniqueness and to understand themselves in terms of chimeras such as 'brightness' or 'talent' supposedly innate in certain individuals. In fact 'brightness' and 'talent' are developed as alienable forms of mental labour. Nevertheless, the aspirations toward self-expression, like those toward 'cooperation', continually threaten to go beyond the specific form they take within capitalist production. While these tendencies are more pronounced among highly educated sectors of the work force, the ideology that underlies them is spread to all sectors.

A collective consciousness of great diversity has been created. Experienced personally as individual and unique, it is simultaneously integral to and shaped by capitalist development. Non-marxist thinkers have always understood this development ideologically, abstracting either the pole of personal aloneness or the pole of social control. Their theories of the twentieth century portray either 'mass society', 'other-directed man', 'men without qualities', 'organization man', 'conformism', the 'rise of the masses', or, the polar opposite, 'existential man', 'irrational man', 'psychological man', 'post-industrial' or 'post-scarcity' man, man for whom hell is other people. In fact, developed capitalism has mass-produced specific forms of personal life, and of individuality, which simultaneously reinforce and threaten capitalist hegemony.

Increasingly cut off from production, the contemporary family threatens to become a well of subjectivity divorced from any social meaning. Within it a world of vast psychological complexity has developed as the counterpart to the extraordinary degree of rationalization and impersonality achieved by capital in the sphere of commodity production. The individualist values generated by centuries of bourgeois development – self-consciousness, perfectionism, independence – have taken new shape through the insatiability of personal life in developed capitalist society. The internal life of the family is dominated by a search for personal fulfilment for which there seem to be no rules.* Much of this search has been at the expense of women.

Already in the late nineteenth century American women were consumed with a sense of their own diminished role and stature when compared with their mothers and grandmothers,[71] women who laboured within the productive unity of the family defined by private property. In a letter to Jane Addams in the early twentieth century, Charlotte Gilman described the married woman's sense of living second-hand, of getting life in translation, of finding oneself unready and afraid in the 'face of experience'.[72] By 1970 this fear had become a desperate sense of loss. Meredith Tax describes the 'limbo of private time and space' of the housewife:

> When I am by myself, I am nothing. I only know that I exist because I am needed by someone who is real, my husband, and by my children. My husband goes out into the real world . . . I stay in the imaginary world in this house, doing jobs that I largely invent, and that no one cares about but myself. . . . I seem to be involved in some sort of mysterious process.[73]

---

* Asked for an explanation for the proliferation of clinics for sex therapy William Masters (of Masters and Johnson) gave as one reason 'a man and a woman need each other more now than ever before. People need someone to hold on to. Once they had the clan but now they only have each other.' *New York Times*, 29 October 1972.

74

Just as the rise of industry in the eighteenth and nine-teenth centuries cut women off from men and gave a new meaning to male supremacy, so the rise of mass education has created the contemporary form of youth and adolescence. The 'generation gap' is the result of the family lagging behind the dominant tendencies of the culture and of the trans-formation of productive skills which children learn in school and through the media. Parents now appear 'stupid' and 'backward' to their children, representing, as they do, an earlier stage of capitalist development. Beginning in the early twentieth century the family began to appear to young people as a prison cut off from reality.*

At the same time, in the form of 'public opinion', the imperatives of capitalist production have been recreated with-in the family, particularly in the 'expectations' through which parents bludgeon themselves and their children into submis-sion.† Fathers, like school teachers or policemen, appear to stand for the whole bourgeois order. Hence, the split between the public and the private is recreated within the family. As in the 'outside world', people feel they are not known for them-selves, not valued for who they really are.

While serving as a refuge, personal life has also become depersonalized; subjective relations tend to become dis-engaged, impersonal, and mechanically determined. Intro-

---

* At this point, 'What is the meaning of life?' becomes a pervasive question among youth. Eugene Gant in *Look Homeward Angel* is a good example.

† Aaron Esterson, *The Leaves of Spring*, Harmondsworth 1970, a study of a schizophrenic family, distinguishes between 'public opinion' which dominates the family's collective life and 'God' who operates primarily when the individual is alone, especially in the toilet, the only room within the family in which privacy actually prevails.

spection has promised to open a new world to men and women, but increasingly the inner life reverberates with the voices of others, the imperatives of social production. This is inevitable because the expansion of inner and personal life has been as integral to capitalist expansion in the modern epoch as has the spread of capitalism throughout the world.

But this process has also given shape to the revolutionary possibilities of our time. In previous centuries only a handful of individuals were prized for their special qualities of mind or character; the mass of men and women were ground down to an approximate sameness in the general struggle for existence. What distinguishes developed capitalist society is that the stress on individual development and uniqueness has become a tendency characterizing all of society.

The bourgeoisie made its revolution on behalf of a specific property form – private property – which it already possessed. But the only 'property' that the proletariat possesses lies within itself: our inner lives and social capabilities, our dreams, our desires, our fears, our sense of ourselves as interconnected beings. Reflecting the 'separation' of personal life from production, a new idea has emerged on a mass scale: that of human relations, and human beings, as an end in themselves.

This idea as it currently prevails is ideological. It presents human beings as an end in themselves only insofar as they are abstracted from the labour process. These ideas flourish within the worlds of modern art, psychology, and communes, and in such utopian authors as Norman O. Brown who envision a society passing totally beyond the realm of necessity. But in themselves they cannot supply the basis for a transformation of society, since a new society – whether socialist, communist, or anarchist – would necessarily be based upon a new organization of labour and a new mode of production.

But these ideas also express what is realistic: the possibility of a society in which the production of necessary goods is a subordinate part of social life and in which the purposes and character of labour are determined by the needs of the individual members of society. It is appropriate that the family, in which so many of the most universal and impelling material processes of society have so far taken place, should also indicate the limited ability of capitalism to subordinate human needs to its own empty aggrandizement. The latest and most democratic form of an old hope can be discerned in the often tortured relations of contemporary personal life: that humanity can pass beyond a life dominated by relations of production. In varying forms this hope has given shape to radical and revolutionary movements since the nineteenth century.

5.
Politics and Personal Life

As the rise of industrial capitalism progressively removed goods production from the home, men and women came to see the family as separate from the economy, and personal life as a separate sphere of life divorced from the larger society. Revolutionary movements against capitalism have tended to recreate this separation through their failure to challenge it. The most recent – and extreme – expression of this tendency has been the polarization between radical feminism and traditional American socialist and communist politics.

Radical feminism, as presented in Firestone's *Dialectic of Sex*, identifies the root cause of war, exploitation and racism as the 'power psychology', the ceaseless striving to dominate others, that originates in the rule of men within the family. Economic exploitation, which marxists identify as the motor of history, is merely one form of domination. For Firestone the family operates independently of the economy; by shaping the psychological life of men and women it shapes the economy and the rest of society. Unlike previous movements which focused on outward manifestations of social control such as the economy or the state, radical feminism would go deeper and transform men and women directly.

The American Communist Party and most other socialist organizations have stood at the opposite pole from radical feminism. These groups have focused on the immediate relations of workers and capitalists within the sphere of commodity production to the exclusion of other areas of society.

They have assigned women a secondary role within the social-ist movement, except insofar as they were members of the working class, and have downgraded the radical feminist attention to family life as a 'petit-bourgeois' or 'subjective' preoccupation. Personal life and the family, they argued, would be changed more or less automatically through a revolution within the sphere of commodity production.

As I have sought to show, this polarization is rooted in the social structure of developed capitalist society and it may be useful at this point to recapitulate the argument already made. Firestone portrays the division between women in the family and men in the economy as a natural or biological condition that antedates history; in fact it arose at a relatively recent stage of capitalist development. Until the rise of in-dustry both personal life and commodity production were organized within a family unit based upon private property. In the United States, because of the relatively wide diffusion of small private property, this way of life was particularly pervasive and persistent. White Americans and, after the Civil War, black Americans too, continually aspired to be small, independent, property-owning producers – farmers, shopkeepers, home manufacturers, mechanics and artisans who owned their own tools. As in Europe, this ideal was always belied by the bourgeoisie that inspired it. Beginning in the colonial settlements, American capitalists forced small producers into economic dependence. By 1840 the rise of the New England textile industry had socialized a major form of women's domestic labour. Throughout the nineteenth century industrial capital spread into the South and West. Nevertheless, the ideal of competitive individualism was sus-tained through economic and territorial expansion, which Americans came to see as natural – just as private property was natural. As a result the transformation caused by proletarianization occurred later than in Europe and has been particularly drastic. Even though by 1870 two out of every three productively engaged Americans, excluding housewives, were hired workers,[74] many of these workers were close to artisan status and could expect to own property. And employers were small and rural and, in contrast to the big merchants and financiers, were often grouped together with their employees under the term 'free labour'.

During the last third of the nineteenth century, and particularly after 1890, the slow inevitable tendencies of capitalist development produced a qualitative transformation. American society polarized between a small, centralized bourgeoisie in control of the 'trusts' and a mass of dispossessed proletarians who owned only their own labour-power and household goods. By World War I, the emerging corporate capitalist class had won the American people to a new epoch. Such phrases as 'the end of American innocence' and 'America's coming of age' symbolize the acquiescence of Americans in the demise of private productive property and their entry into a vast army of labour that, every morning, goes to work, and evenings and weekends, recovers from it.

This same transformation gave rise to a new form of the family, one with no apparent connection to the rest of society. The production of exchange value was removed from the family and vested in large-scale, 'impersonal' corporate units. But rather than destroying traditional bourgeois family life this transformation gave it a new meaning as the realm of happiness, love, and individual freedom. With the rise of corporate capitalism, the family became the major institution in society given over to the personal needs of its members. Society divided between an inner and an outer world. At one pole the individual was central and a sometimes desperate search for warmth, intimacy, and mutual support prevailed.

At the other pole social relations were anonymous and coerced; the individual was reduced to an interchangeable economic unit.

This same transformation mystified and obscured the place of the housewife within capitalist production. The specific class position of the housewife under capitalism now lay in her 'classlessness' – i.e., the absence of a direct relation to the capitalist class.[75] Socialists and others understood her class position to be that of her husband, since her relation to the outside world was mediated through him. But the creation of a separate sphere of personal life among the proletariat entailed the creation of a separate class of housewives and mothers whose physical and mental labour reproduced this separate sphere. In contrast to the proletarian who worked in large socialized units and received a wage, the housewife worked alone and was unpaid. Rather than working for a corporation the housewife worked for a particular man, for herself, and for their children and relatives. Housework and child-rearing came to be seen as natural or personal functions performed in some private space outside society.

Twentieth-century socialist movements failed to challenge this ideological view of personal life and of women's labour within the home. The basis for this ideology is in seeing production and the economy as restricted to the sphere of commodity production and exchange. According to Marx, any society, if it is to survive, requires that its members organize themselves into a system of social production in order to meet their basic material needs. The form in which social labour is distributed changes from society to society and is determined by the dominant mode of production. Capitalist production takes the form of the production of surplus value. The fact that housewives and mothers do not produce surplus value has obscured their participation with wage labour in an inter-dependent system of production. Thus, when socialists spoke of the economy as the determining force in society and restricted the meaning of economy to the sphere of surplus value, they lost the sense of capitalism as an integrated social system.

Because they excluded the family from their conception of capitalist production, socialists could not distinguish the specific oppression of women from the general oppression of the working class. Focusing on the rise of industry and the growth of the proletariat they missed its complement. - the isolation of housewives and children from socialized production and the emergence of a separate sphere of personal life that veiled women's labour in the home. Every programme developed by socialists for female liberation depended upon the entry of women into the wage labour force. Similarly, feminists, before the emergence of the current women's movement, sought to liberate women through an emphasis on jobs, equal pay, education, and, above all, through the ballot. The result, as in the Russian Revolution or in early twentieth century American feminism, has been to transform the position of women as wage labourers and professionals or in political life, while leaving women's place within the family relatively intact. Socialist movements have also lost touch with the development of modern personal life. Excluding the family from their conception of social production, socialists tended to accept the ideological portrayal of personal life that prevails in bourgeois society - that personal life is an entirely subjective phenomenon, having meaning only for the individual.

Against and outside the twentieth-century socialist movement an important modern tradition has developed based upon the emergence of a sphere of personal life not directly subordinate to capital. Utopians, hippies, existentialists, bohemians, psychoanalytically oriented radicals, communitarians, and sexual freedom advocates have stressed the key role of inner psychological change and of immediate personal relations in transcending if not transforming society. These currents have tended to distrust socialism in particular and politics in general as superficial or external responses to problems they see as rooted more deeply in the human condition. This is a tradition upon which radical feminism drew and against which it has fought. In common with this tradition radical feminism attempts to defend the personal and restore trust in subjectivity. But against psychoanalysis and similar currents radical feminism insists upon the necessity of waging a systematic political struggle.

But the radical feminist defence of subjectivity has not challenged, but assumed, the view of the family and personal life as a separate sphere ruled by its own laws. Rather than viewing the contemporary family as specific to developed capitalism, radical feminism takes it to be a universal form of oppression. 'Beneath economics', wrote Firestone, 'reality is psychosexual'. Marxism's failure was that 'it did not dig deep enough to the psychosexual roots of class'.[76] These roots were the domination of women by men and of children by adults, essentially within the family. Basing its politics on the predominance of women within the personal sphere, radical feminism leaves uncontested the capitalist domination of society as a whole.

While the opposition between radical feminism and socialism is rooted in the divided structure of capitalist society, it was not inevitable that political movements would recapitulate this division. This chapter is a history of how the division developed. In the nineteenth century, socialists envisioned a revolution that would transform every area of life. This was clearest among utopian socialists who based much of their outlook upon the petty bourgeois family in which production and personal life were still integrated. Nineteenth-century individualism and utopian socialism defended the whole individual against the fragmentation of capitalist society. Similarly, marxian socialists understood themselves to be extending the limited political democracy achieved by the bourgeois revolutions (particularly the French Revolution) to the 'private' economic realm of civil society and the family. Throughout most of the nineteenth century the relation between commodity production and the rest of society had not yet become problematic and veiled. In Europe and the United States the question of the emancipation of women played a much larger part in the nineteenth and early twentieth century socialist movements than it has since the Russian Revolution. In the United States, currents of artistic modernism, bohemia, and sexual freedom were more closely associated with socialism before the 1920s than after. This was a period in which radicals anticipated an imminent social revolution.

In the United States the split between the traditions of personal liberation and of social transformation began to occur in the early twentieth century. The rise of corporate capitalism led to the emergence of forms of personal life that were seen as independent of the mode of production. The split was accelerated by the domination of the American left by the Soviet Union and the emergence of a model of socialism based simply on the planned expansion of goods production. Currents based upon the new sphere of personal life such as psychoanalysis and bohemia tended to play down or ignore the importance of the economy. For this reason the communist movement has downgraded these currents as 'petit-bourgeois' or 'middle class'. But the idea that personal life would be transformed automatically through the transformation of production had its major relevance in pre-industrial societies like Russia and China where the family as a whole was still a unit of commodity production. The development of corporate capitalism in the United States, where the overwhelming majority of the population depends on wages in order to survive, entails the development of a separate personal life. This in turn sets new tasks for a socialist movement – tasks that the Communist Party barely began to address, and that have only recently begun to take political form.

The politics of individualism: Charles Fourier

The defence of the individual against capitalism began amid the petty bourgeois movements of artisans, peasants, and tradesmen opposed to the rise of large-scale capital in the early nineteenth century. Within these movements the defence of small-scale private property was often inter-mingled with a defence of the individual as an end in him- or herself. Since private property and the self-sufficient family were the bases of these movements the split between the personal and the political was not part of their outlook. Utopian socialists, reformers, and radical artists in the period following the French Revolution discussed morality and the family as easily as politics and economics.[77] They saw the enhancement of the individual as the end of political change, and saw the individual's self-transformation as its means. The Marquis de Sade, whose personal and sexual experiments represent one of the many blind alleys of the new individualism, articulated a widely felt sentiment: 'Frenchmen! You are too enlightened not to feel that a new government will necessitate a new way of living.'[78] A similar emphasis underlies transcendentalism, communalism,

85

abolitionism, civil disobedience, educational reform, perfectionism, and the campaigns of moral suasion of the Jacksonian United States.

Many of the liberating potentialities of early nineteenth century individualism as well as its limitations can be seen in the work of Charles Fourier, who, writing during and after the French Revolution, produced an extraordinarily comprehensive critique of capitalist society on behalf of a new conception of the individual and the possibilities of social life. Against the competitive egotism based upon private property upheld by the prevailing Jacobin ideology, Fourier argued that men and women were emotional beings who expressed themselves through social interaction. In common with the romantic poets Fourier affirmed the subjective self, but unlike them he never ceased to stress that the self could only be realized with and through others. As with the romantics, the basis of Fourier's outlook was the conflict between 'human nature' or 'the individual' and society.

While every individual was unique, Fourier argued, all individual character developed through the combination of a limited number of basic passions, which 'remain invariable among all nations of men'.* Under the reign of 'civilization', Fourier's term for competitive capitalism, the natural impulses of men and women were repressed and distorted by 'morality', the mortal enemy of 'passional attraction'. People

---

* The passions range from those arising from the senses to love, ambition, friendship, and consanguinity to the passion for intrigue, complexity, variety, and the desire to share one's life with others. These go through endless permutations. Charles Fourier, *Design for Utopia*, New York 1971. All quotations from Fourier are from this book unless otherwise noted. Mark Poster's 'Fourier's Concept of the Group' (unpublished manuscript) was also of great help to me.

were forced into constant warfare with themselves so they might conform to some bloodless ideal. Fourier argued that a passion was neither good nor bad in itself. Any passion might be beneficial in the proper social combination. Society must be organized in self-sufficient communities designed to enhance the expression and combination of the passions. To advance this goal, Fourier compiled an obsessive catalogue of social needs and instinctual passions – a 'calculus of passional attraction'. For instance, he would capitalise on children's attraction to dirt by having them manage the community's waste.

In such a society, production and consumption would not be severed, as in capitalism, but would be unified. In this way, human needs would dictate economic development: 'Our starting point is that a general perfection in industry will be attained by the universal demands and refinement of the consumers.' Agriculture under civilization, for example, is onerous labour partly because 'people are too poor to participate in the consumption of choice foods'.* At the same time, 'the epicure is not a cultivator, his epicurism lacks a *direct* bond with cultivation; it is nothing but sensuality'.[79] In the future state of civilisation, production would be guided by the 'generalization of epicureanism' while consumption would be an integrated part of active social life.

Fourier's commitment to communities that would unify the personal and social needs of people is related to his unusual sensitivity to the problems of the family and to the

---

* Fourier's range is indicated by his unusual sensitivity to the importance of eating in daily life: 'Questions regarding love and gourmandise are treated facetiously by the Civilized, who do not understand the importance that God attaches to our pleasures.' Jonathan Beecher and Richard Bienvenu, *The Utopian Vision of Charles Fourier*, Boston 1972, p.265.

oppression of women. While some utopian socialists exalted the petty bourgeois family and its 'natural' division of labour,* others, like Fourier and the Saint-Simonians, advocated free love or other measures as a means of attacking traditional patriarchy. In this way the cause of the emancipation of women came to be linked, in the early nineteenth century, with the defence of individualism against the bourgeois ideal of the family.[80]

Fourier wrote that the 'extension of privileges to women is the general principle of all social progress'. His main charge against the French Revolution was its failure to abolish the family. A travelling salesman and a bachelor, Fourier wrote, 'I have witnessed closely many families. I have not found a single one joyful on the inside ... In general, every family seems to say, like Dido: I want to flee, I want to escape from myself.'[81] The bourgeois family 'brought domestic society to the highest degree of isolation and egoism by dividing it into sexual couples or exclusive married households. Would it be possible to push unsociability farther?'[82] Sexuality, to which Fourier assigned a central place in human life,† was trapped and deformed by the family. The central problem of the utopian communities of the early nineteenth century became on one hand 'the extension of family union beyond the little man-and-wife circle to large corporations' and, on the other, 'whether the existence of the marital family is compatible with that of the universal family, which the term "Community" signifies'.[83]

---

*For example, Proudhon: 'Marriage is the union of two heterogeneous elements, *power* and *grace*.' *Selected Writings*, New York 1969, p.254.

†Voluptuousness is the sole arm which God can employ to master us and lead us to carry out his designs; he rules the universe *by Attraction and not by Force*.' *Design*, p.61.

Fourier's work indicates the psychological range and depth of early nineteenth century individualism, as well as the limitations of an outlook that takes the individual, rather than an overall conception of social development, as its starting point. Fourier brilliantly attacks the repression, guilt, and narrow egotism characteristic of competitive capitalism[84] but he does so on the basis of an abstract conception of human nature that ends paradoxically by replicating the bourgeois individualism he abhors. In emphasizing the emotions and criticizing bourgeois morality Fourier goes far beyond the calculating individualism of Jacobinism, but his model of human nature remains the isolated family working a piece of private property on which personal and economic life are integrated. Fourier would simply extend this mode of life to include a large number and variety of communitarians. His conception of socialist property relations is really that of private property shared by the community – as private property is shared within the family. Moreover, the passions that Fourier takes as permanent and unchanging – love, ambition, intrigue – are the frustrated social relations of competitive capitalist society; Fourier proposes to fulfil them through association, rather than to criticize and transform them. Indeed, the Fourierist phalanxes, like other utopian communities, invariably reproduced the social relations of the society they sought to escape. Fourier's view of human nature is necessarily dualistic; the passions rise upward from men and women while civilization thwarts and distorts them from above. He calls for a society in which needs dictate economic development but does not recognize that economic development has already dictated particular needs.

Fourier's commitment to the individual or 'human nature', abstracted from its class position, gives his work great force. He reminds us that all people are 'poor' under capitalism, whatever class they belong to. Their desires are unfulfilled, their senses stunted, their complex social sensibilities pitifully constricted. But the same vision severely limits the scope of Fourier's conception of revolution. For Fourier, socialism will be achieved through small bands of believers who take deliberate and purposeful control of their immediate social relations. From the point of view of petty bourgeois private property it would make no sense to call that an 'individual' solution. So long as private productive property remained dispersed, all solutions were individual.

Friedrich Engels and the politics of class

Fourier's vision of a world organized around the emotional and sensual relations of men and women at first glance contrasts sharply with Marx and Engels' consistent focus on the outer historical world of politics and economics. Yet when Engels considered the question of the family in *The Origin of the Family, Private Property and the State*, he originally intended to place Fourier's 'brilliant critique of civilization' side by side with his own historical account.[85]

By the time Marx and Engels began their collaboration, utopian socialism had devolved into a series of squabbling sects. In attempting to provide a theoretical and political basis for the romantic critique of capitalism, Marx and Engels discovered the role of commodity production and class relations in determining the character of all other social relations, and of the working class as the only group capable of making the revolution. This gave marxian socialists a unified perspective that other social movements lacked. Engels' *Origin of the Family*, written in 1884 and incorporating Marx's notes, is the major marxist attempt to situate the family, and the oppression of women, in relation to the historical development of production. According to Engels, personal oppression within the family results from its place within a mode of production based upon private property and class divisions.

Primitive society, Engels argues, was characterized by organic unity. The gens or primitive community was simultaneously family and society. Membership was through kinship; property was held in common. Engels links the emergence of the family to the emergence of the state.* In primitive society no separate 'public' sphere stood over and above the members of society.

> There was as yet no distinction between [private] rights and [public] duties; the question of whether participation in public affairs, blood revenge or atonement for injuries was a right or a duty never confronted the Indian; it would have appeared as absurd to him as the question of whether eating, sleeping or hunting was a right or a duty.[86]

In such a society, the fact that women had responsibility for child-rearing and for the household economy signified not their oppression but, in Engels' words, their 'free' and 'highly respected' position. The household economy 'was just as much a public, a socially necessary industry as the providing of food by the men'.[87] Engels concludes:

> That woman was the slave of man at the commencement of society is one of the most absurd notions that have come down to us from the period of the Enlightenment of the eighteenth century.[88]

According to Engels, woman's oppression arose through the creation of a separate sphere of private life – the 'family' –

---

* Similarly, Marx wrote: 'The abstraction of the state as such was not born until the modern era, because the abstraction of private life was not created until the modern era.' 'Critique of Hegel's Doctrine of the State' in *Early Writings*, New York 1975, p.90.

based upon the private appropriation of communal property. Private property was made possible by the production of a surplus above what was immediately necessary to sustain life. Engels is vague in describing this transformation, but he stresses the emergence of new productive forces (particularly domesticated animals) that could not be contained within the limited social structure of the household-centred gens. Traditional kinship ties now began to break down as families separated off from the gens, basing their new identity on private property. Engels implies, but does not explain, that 'private property' had its own dynamic of expansion. For example, slavery now developed, made possible since labour could now produce more than its cost of maintenance.

The rise of private property spelled the downfall of women. Production outside the household expanded far more rapidly than production within the household. As a result the traditional division of labour between men and women, which had arisen out of the physiological differences between the sexes, took on a new social meaning. As the household dwindled in importance, so too did the role of women. In the gens kinship had been matrilineal, but men now sought to overthrow traditional kinship forms so that property could be preserved within the 'private' family. Engels calls the development of patrilineal kinship the 'world-historic defeat of the female sex'. Basing himself upon the ownership of property, 'the man seized the reins in the house also, the woman was degraded, enthralled, the slave of man's lust, a mere instrument for breeding children'.[89] 'The wife became the first domestic servant pushed out of participation in social production.'[90] Her oppression was fixed by her restriction to the household. Away from women arose the state, 'a special public authority separated from the totality of those concerned'.[91] Its purpose was 'to safeguard the newly acquired property of private individuals against the communistic traditions of the gentile order'.[92] The existence of the state was an admission that society had 'become entangled in an insoluble contradiction with itself'.[93]

Since the domestic sphere is based wholly upon private property, Engels would end the oppression of women by abolishing private property. 'The predominance of the man in marriage', he writes, 'is simply a consequence of his economic predominance and will vanish with it automatically'.[94] Politically this involved a dual programme. 'Private housekeeping', along with child-raising, must be 'transformed into a social industry'. Conversely, the spread of industry into the family was to be accompanied by the entry of women into industry: 'The emancipation of women becomes possible only when women are enabled to take part in production on a large, social scale.'[95]

The Origin of the Family has often been criticized for its inconsistencies, unilinear historical scheme, and factual inaccuracies.[96] While these criticisms are valid, they do not dispel the power of Engels' work. As a historical speculation on the origins of class society *The Origin of the Family* successfully ties together the oppression of women and the existence of the family with the economic organization of society.* The book's major theoretical weakness lies in tracing the oppression of women to private property in general, without any attempt to indicate that both private property and women's oppression have different meanings in different modes of production. In fact, what Engels has done

---

* *The Origin of the Family* can be viewed as an attempt to describe the basic character of human history by a sort of myth of its origins. It can be compared to Freud's *Totem and Taboo* in this regard. Another related book, far more historical, is Fustel de Coulanges, *The Ancient City* (1864).

is to project the split between socialized production and the family, as it developed under capitalism, back upon all previous society. In doing so he fails to be specific about either the impact of *capitalist* private property or the continuous, and continuously changing, ideology and structure of male supremacy.

As a result, Engels fails to specify the place of women, as housewives and mothers, in relation to capitalist production. Although in his preface to *The Origin of the Family* Engels portrays the family in all societies as an integral part of the mode of production, he never returns to this critical insight.* While he terms the family the 'economic unit' of society, he restricts this term to its role in the transmission of private property. He reinforces the bourgeois equation of production with the production of surplus value, and of work with wage labour, and therefore portrays women's labour within the home as marginal to society. This idea reinforces the exclusion of housewives and mothers, and their concerns, from socialist politics.

Engels wrote at a time when the proletarian family had not yet been stabilized and when its life was dominated by the struggle for survival. Changes in the nature of the family and of society since then raise additional problems. Writing before a separate sphere of personal life had emerged within the

---

* Engels wrote: 'According to the materialistic conception, the determining factor in history is, in the last resort, the production and reproduction of immediate life. But this itself is of a twofold character. On the one hand, the production of the means of subsistence ... on the other, the production of human beings themselves, the propagation of the species. ... Social institutions ... are conditioned by both kinds of production: by the stage of development of labour, on the one hand, and of the family, on the other.' *Origin*, pp.170–71.

proletariat, Engels does not examine the ideological, psychological, and emotional life of the family. For Engels private property is the material reality upon which the family exists as a subjective contingency. Engels was convinced that proletarian family life was being obliterated by the rise of capital. His description of the family is bare and external, as if the inner, subjective life of the family either did not exist or was of little consequence.

In addition, Engels does not challenge the natural or biological basis of the family insofar as it has persisted into the present.[97] That basis is the sexual division of labour – for example, the responsibility of women for child care – and heterosexuality. Heterosexuality is the precondition for the sexual division of labour; the division of labour, by insuring the reciprocal dependence of the sexes, gives rise to the 'bias toward heterosexuality'. Engels portrays the sexual division of labour as a natural or spontaneous phenomenon that derives its oppressive meaning only through the growth of commodity production. He assumes that under socialism the family will embody the traditional division of labour (to the extent that its productive functions have not been fully socialized) and that it will be based upon heterosexuality. But the development of contraception, changes in the technology of reproduction, and the declining need for labourers make it possible to challenge the original biological imperatives.[98] Engels accepts the perpetuation of natural conditions into a period when they are no longer compelling.

These weaknesses influence Engels' solution. He would resolve the contradiction between women and men simply by integrating women into the industrial proletariat; he would eliminate the contradiction between the family and the economy by industrializing the functions of the home. Engels was right to emphasize the centrality of the sphere of socialized production, but wrong in believing that changes within this sphere would necessarily transform, as if by reflex, the sphere of private and family life. Entry into modern industrial production did bestow a certain independence upon working women in relation to men, but rather than eliminating oppression within the family this independence exacerbated and deepened the contradiction between the 'public' and 'private' spheres of life. Engels' account encourages the view that the social relations of personal life can be transformed without selfconscious political struggle. He did not believe that the psychological life of the family, its ancestral division of labour, and its historically developed sentiments and emotional relations could persist through a transformation of the mode of production. He believed that male supremacy will 'vanish automatically' along with its original cause – private property. His vision of emancipation is rooted in the nineteenth-century proletarian family's struggle for survival. He assumes that under socialism the functions currently performed by the family will be socialized, but that something very much like the bourgeois family, based upon individual sex love and embodying the sexual division of labour, will flourish.

Within the socialist movement Engels' book was taken not as a beginning but as the final word. Within the Second International women's entry into the labour force determined their role in the revolution. The needs of women were thereby assimilated to the needs of the industrial proletariat. Domesticity, wrote Rosa Luxemburg, 'is but the private affair of the worker, his happiness and blessing, and for this reason non-existent for our present society'.[99] Not only was women's labour within the home considered marginal, but so were all other 'private' concerns. In his famous conversation with Clara Zetkin, Lenin expressed dismay at what he considered bourgeois influence on socialist women: 'I have been told that at the evenings arranged for reading and discussion with working women, sex and marriage problems came first . . . I could not believe my ears when I heard that.'[100] The solitary emphasis on production allowed party members to remain staunchly puritanical while spurning the hypocrisy of the Victorian bourgeoisie. Free love, and other varieties of sexual reform, were relegated to the tradition of 'personal emancipation'. Along with Engels socialists assumed that the only problem with the working-class family was that it was driven by economic necessity and that under socialism the family based upon love would automatically come into its own.[101]

Russia and China:
Revolution based upon economic development
Both the strengths and the weaknesses of Engels' theory of the family can be seen in the Russian and Chinese revolutions. In Russia and China, the transformation of the family, and of the oppression of women, has been both a consequence and a component of the overall development of the productive forces. Both revolutions began by destroying feudal and slave social relations, in which women were mired, in order to create a relatively egalitarian and homogeneous body of citizens and workers. The establishment of legal equality through marriage and divorce codes, the abolition of polygamy, and other reforms, along with the entry of women into industry, raised women in both countries from a position close to slavery to membership in the working class. Hence the early phases of these revolutions accomplished a transformation that Engels expected capitalism to perform. 'Industry', Lenin wrote in an early study, 'creates a new position for the woman in

which she is completely independent of her family and husband . . . This is the equality of the proletarian.'[102]

Soviet policy since the revolution has been based on the principle that women and family life would be liberated through the development of production. In the early years of the revolution the Bolsheviks promulgated the most advanced programme of European and American feminism: abolition of ecclesiastical marriage; women's right to property, legal abortion, and contraception; marriage and divorce codes based upon the equality of men and women; recognition of de facto marriage; and equal rights for illegitimate children. They regarded these measures as part of the bourgeois phase of their revolution, recognizing that these rights were purely formal. Real equality would come through the entry of women into the labour force and thereby into political life.

While ideas concerning free love, the 'new woman', and the abolition of the family were initially important, especially in the cities, such concerns had begun to be postponed or downgraded by the 1920s as diversions from the single-minded focus on economic growth. Russian marxists and earlier intellectuals had introduced the romantic tradition of personal liberation into a country in which a separate sphere of personal life scarcely existed except among the aristocracy and bourgeoisie. While most Bolsheviks felt that the family, like the state, would eventually 'wither away', this was not a subject of mass political discussion. As Trotsky wrote in 1923:

> The party did not and could not afford specific attention to questions of the everyday life of the working masses. . . . We have never thrashed out these questions . . . as we have the questions of wages, fines, the length of the working day, police prosecution, the form of the state, the ownership of land and so on.[103]

During the period of War Communism problems of acute food shortages and homeless children led to the establishment of collective dining, nurseries, and settlements.[104] Hence the pressures of material survival contributed to the belief that the family was being abolished. But by the NEP period the reconstruction of domestic life, after its devastation by war and revolution, was valued more highly than experiments in collective living.[105] By the 1930s, while the question of the family remained a major social question, the European heritage of 'personal liberation' had been completely eliminated from Soviet life.*

Soviet policy went beyond the romantic concern with the family as a moral issue and began to make explicit the role of the family in economic life. State planning of the family was integrated with and subordinated to economic planning, population policy, and the control of crime. In 1935 the Soviet government sought to strengthen traditional family life by making abortion and divorce more difficult and by forbidding homosexuality. A major purpose was to utilize the labour of grandmothers for child-rearing in order that both parents might work. In addition the government sought to raise the birth rate to strengthen the Soviet position in world politics.[106] World War II and twenty million dead added the special problem of re-peopling the country; in 1944 the

---

* The idea that Bolshevik policy during the 1930s represented a radical reversal probably arose with Wilhelm Reich's *The Sexual Revolution*, New York 1972, first published in 1945, and has been popularized in Kate Millett's *Sexual Politics*, New York 1970. There was certainly change but there was also an underlying continuity. The conservative counterpart to Reich's polemic is the academic opinion that the Bolsheviks first attempted to abolish the family, and then learned it couldn't be done.

formal bonds of the family were further strengthened to counter its wartime dissolution.

The social transformation accomplished in Russia is similar to the path traversed by capitalist development over the past two centuries: universal proletarianization and the rise of large-scale industry. One result of this transformation has been a split between public and private life comparable to the one that prevails in developed capitalist society. But the private or personal sphere, rather than being idealized as in the West, has been downgraded; the state continually intrudes upon the 'autonomy' of the family, eroding its promise of comfort, privacy, and individual freedom. Much of the current protest activity in the Soviet Union is in part an appeal for the enhancement of the private sphere: personal liberty; increased consumption; freedom of speech, travel, artistic expression, etc. For the first time in Soviet history there is a social basis for these demands.

The Bolshevik revolution began with a deep commitment to the emancipation of women. The eventual limits of that emancipation are instructive. The tradition of personal liberation had little meaning in a pre-industrial society in which the family was still the basic hub of production, and in which production and personal life were integrated. It was difficult for the Bolsheviks to see whether and in what form personal life could become a progressive political issue. Soffia N. Smidovich, a feminist and Bolshevik, explained: 'We are inclined . . . to close our eyes about a lot, when the matter concerns so-called personal life . . . We are apprehensive lest we fall into dogmatism, carry on like the priests, and so on.'[107] Nor was the tradition of personal liberation, free love, and abolition of the family integrated with a commitment to feminism. As in Europe and the United States, personal liberation and sexual freedom primarily benefited men. During

100

the Russian revolution this was known as the 'mutuality problem'. The ease of divorce, for example, when children were involved meant 'the women remains tied with chains to the ... ruins of the family hearth. The man, happily whistling, can leave it'.[108] In this context, it was seen as possible to reconcile the strengthening of the traditional family with the goal of emancipating women.

Revolution through economic development left intact a major part of women's oppression. The psychosocial heritage of male supremacy was scarcely challenged by the entry of women into industry, while the strengthening of the family encouraged a resurgence of traditional patriarchal ideals, such as the exaltation of motherhood.* Perhaps most important, the division of labour within the family retained all its force; as Firestone wrote, 'the roles of women were enlarged rather than redefined'.[109] Because housework and child-rearing had never been granted full status as forms of social production, the commitment to equality never extended to labour performed within the home. This in turn restricted the attack on the sexual division of labour in industry. The emancipation of women in the Soviet Union has been subordinated to the overall development of the productive forces. Women benefited from their proletarianization and from the general betterment of life, but the issue of women's liberation, as a separate issue, was eliminated from Soviet politics.

The Chinese and Russian revolutions share many similarities. As in the Soviet Union, the Chinese communists destroyed feudal and slave kinship relations that the Chinese

---

* The ideal of motherhood was associated with the re-emergence of Great Russian nationalism and the idea of the 'Motherland' during the 1930s.

bourgeoisie had only challenged. Chinese communism abolished wife purchase, footbinding, polygamy, concubinage, and ancestor worship, and put in their place monogamous marriage based upon the free choice of man and woman. As in the Soviet Union, the party stresses the entry of women into social production as the key to their emancipation. The emphasis on women's equality has waxed and waned in relation to overall questions of economic development.

During periods in which the Chinese followed the Soviet plan of development – hierarchical division of labour, relatively greater stress on material incentives, capital-intensive production, and an emphasis on developing heavy industry – the issue of women's liberation has been played down and women have even been encouraged to remain in the home. But the Chinese have also learned from the inadequacies of the Soviet model. Beginning with the Great Leap Forward (which was in part prompted by the Hungarian revolution of 1956), the Chinese communists have periodically stressed the integration of economic development with the creation of anti-authoritarian social relations. In such periods the Chinese encouraged labour-intensive industry, the creation of more egalitarian social relations in industry, and the development of medium and light industry in the countryside. As part of the effort to mobilize all available labour power, the Chinese stressed the participation of women in social production. Similarly, support for birth control has been associated with the entry of women into production as well as with the equality of women.[110] The different character of Chinese economic policy in these periods has accented the issue of women's liberation and is one reason for the relatively deeper and more thoroughgoing transformation of the family in the course of the Chinese revolution.

Another difference between the Russian and the Chinese experience lies in the greater importance attached to culture and ideology in the Chinese revolution. Colonial revolutions against imperialism have generally paid much attention to the culture or way of life of the people. Stokely Carmichael represented many third world revolutionaries when he wrote,

> Colonization is not just the economic raping of someone, not merely taking a lot of money away. Colonization deals with destroying the person's language, his history, his identification, his total humanity.[111]

Contact with imperialism throws the traditional culture on the defensive and forces the revolutionary movement either to defend or to supplant it. Family relations and the position of women are integral to the traditional culture of any colonial nation.* But particularly in China the family was at the centre of a highly coherent and deeply rooted social philosophy that united all aspects of traditional society. According to Confucianism, the traditional culture of China, society was organized through a set of five primary relations: father-son, sovereign-minister, husband-wife, old-young, and friendship.[112] The place of the family was closely tied to the world position of China, the role of the emperor, and the authority of the gentry – all social relations challenged by the

---

* This has often encouraged a defence of male supremacy against 'imported Western' ideas such as feminism. For example in Algeria the secretary-general of the FLN has written, 'The way of life of European women is incompatible with our traditions and our culture... We can only live by the Islamic morality'; and an Algerian woman attacking feminism wrote that in the choice between 'the freaks of a super-civilization and . . . tradition, I choose tradition.' David C. Gordon, *Women of Algeria: An Essay on Change*, Cambridge, Mass. 1972, pp.67, 74.

presence of imperialism. The Chinese communists were forced to struggle against this Confucian world view, including its view of the family, in order to supplant the traditional ruling class.

While the Russian revolution was anti-imperialist, Russia was itself an imperialist power. Questions of either preserving or transforming traditional cultural institutions were more important for the subject nationalities freed by the 1917 revolution than for the Soviet nation as a whole. In China, on the other hand, traditional Confucian culture had been forced on the defensive by its inability to resist imperialism for at least a century before the rise of the Communist Party. This was not a debate restricted to the intellectuals but was expressed in a series of mass social movements beginning with the Taiping Rebellion (1853–1868), extending through the Boxer Rebellion (1898–1900) and 4 May Movement (1919), and culminating in the Chinese communists. In all of these movements the viability of Confucianism in the context of imperialism was a continued question. Similarly, conservative movements such as Chiang Kai-shek's argued that Confucianism could continue to serve as a basis of social order. The Western tradition of romantic individualism, free love, and personal liberation played even less role in China than in Russia and was associated with the bourgeois rather than the communist phase of the revolution.[113] But the prolonged struggle against Confucianism has given the question of culture a centrality in the Chinese revolution and helps explain the intensity and persistence with which that question recurs.

Finally, the revolutionary process in China took much longer and penetrated more deeply into the life of the people. In Russia the Bolsheviks took power when they were little known outside the industrial centres. The transformation of society followed the seizure of state power. In China the

104

revolutionary movement ruled large sections of the country for over a decade before winning state power. In this process the integration of village and familial life with socialist production and with party organization was prepared for. Communist production has often accommodated itself to traditional social organization such as the village.[114] This has facilitated the introduction of day care, feeding stations (at work), and other communal institutions. The same writings intended to regulate social production and political life – for example, the Red Book – are read by couples as manuals of family life. There does not seem to be the same tension between public and private space that characterizes developed capitalism and that has emerged in the Soviet Union.[115] Far more than in the Soviet Union, family life has been discussed at political meetings. In fact, the question of women's liberation has come to the fore in periods of mass political participation – such as after the seizure of power and during the Great Leap Forward and the Cultural Revolution – and has receded as political activity has receded.[116]

The Chinese experience, even more than the Soviet, demonstrates the relevance of Engels' emphasis on entry into social production to the emancipation of women. But women in China have had a historically different set of needs than women in the developed capitalist countries. China was an overwhelmingly peasant country in which a separate sphere of personal life had scarcely emerged. In art and in other areas the Chinese have sought to show that the modern Western emphasis on subjective or psychological life is an illusion and that so-called 'personal' questions can be resolved into questions of one's objective class position. For example, in a 1969 attack on Stanislavsky, the Chinese condemn the idea that an actor should act out of inner emotions or project a divided consciousness. Instead, drama should portray the

105

clash of idealized representatives of different classes. Stanislavsky's system, they charge, would replace 'the analysis of objective things with one's subjective imaginary bourgeois feelings'.* In addition sexual life is governed by a puritanism characteristic of countries in the early stage of industrial development. In part this is probably a reaction against the sexual degradation of women in imperial China.[117]

In both Russia and China women have been emancipated as part of the 'emancipation' of the productive forces of society. The basic idea was classic marxism: the social order of the past is destroyed through the expansion of material production. Engels applied this idea to women: male supremacy resulted from the 'backwardness' of the family, its isolation from socialized production. The liberation of women would occur when socialism unblocked the forces of production developed by capitalism, bringing women into industry and industrializing housework. Both Russia and China sought to 'raise' familial life to the level attained by socialist production. Both revolutions have begun to recognize that the family performs critical economic functions which the state can either socialize or reward. The redefinition of the problem of the family from a moral to an economic problem marks a great advance. But as economic problems, questions of the family and of the emancipation of women have been bound by the overall context of material impoverishment. In both countries the vision of 'personal' emancipation – the 'new man', the 'new woman' – has been subsumed by the goal of

* Another charge made against Stanislavsky concerned his reliance on the 'subconscious'. Shanghai Revolutionary Mass Criticism Writing Group, 'On Stanislavsky's "System"', Peking 1969, pp.5, 6, 8, 22.

developing production. The idea of life no longer dominated by relations of production has scarcely emerged.

The emergence of a separate sphere of personal life

In contrast to the Soviet Union and China, Engels' vision of resolving the oppressiveness of the family by revolutionizing the mode of production has appeared less and less plausible in the twentieth-century United States. With the development of industry a sphere of life emerged divorced from any direct relation to social production. By World War I a diverse series of social movements (e.g., family reform), social and psychological milieus (bohemia, 'youth'), and theoretical advances (psychoanalysis) indicated the coming into existence of a new area of social life, the personal. Most Americans continued to see their personal fates as inextricably tied to the development of commodity production; this idea underlay their struggles for better food, shelter, recreation, a shorter workday, education, and culture. At the same time, the rise of corporate capitalism created the possibility of liberating society from the constant constraint of economic necessity. A small but growing number of Americans began to see their personal lives as wholly apart from the sphere of production. In the realm of personal relations, emotional and sexual life, and creative expression, they exercised the 'freedom' denied them within the sphere of alienated labour.

In the nineteenth century, artists and romantic intellectuals proclaimed the emergence of the subjective self, no longer bound by the division of labour. In the early twentieth century, psychologists, educators, progressives, and reformers continued this tradition, reflecting the extension of personal life on a larger social scale. The rise of modern industry centralized private productive property and thus eliminated the economic basis for the patriarchal family. But radicals and reformers held that industrialization was creating a new form of the family based upon the personal freedom of its members. They believed, with Engels, that the entry of women into industry and the industrialization of the productive functions of the family would eliminate the subordination of women. New theories of psychological life, childhood, adolescence, progressive education, and sexuality contributed to a new ideology of personal freedom and individualism based upon wage labour. In this newly discovered realm of personal life Americans in the twentieth century have expressed a constricted vision of freely determined social relations, no longer dominated by the imperatives of production.

Arthur Calhoun, an evolutionary socialist who saw the rise of corporate capitalism as a basically benign step toward socialism, reflected the general optimism of pre-World War I America. 'Industrialism', he wrote, has led to the 'general democratization of society' and the 'waning of domestic monarchy'. As women gained 'economic opportunity outside of marriage', they became freer and more independent within the home. Through her 'formal education, working experience and the development of household economics into a technical pursuit' she confronts man as an equal, and indeed superior, as the man becomes a mere 'earning mechanism'. The passing of society 'into the regime of surplus . . . brings with it the lengthening of infancy and the elevation of childhood'. 'The father cannot comprehend what his children are learning' and so paternal power wanes. 'Society lays claim to the child and refuses to recognize the parent's property right.' 'The family', he concludes, 'experiences individuation, ceases to be a forced grouping, and develops toward ethical unity and spontaneous democracy.'[118]

Charlotte P. Gilman's feminism was based upon a similar analysis. 'The growing individualization of democratic life brings inevitable change to our daughters as well as to our sons', she wrote. Until the rise of industry the family was the basic 'social group, an entity, a little state'. Its basis was economic necessity. In its origins 'it moved over the earth, following its food supply, and fighting occasionally with stranger families for the grass or water on which it depended'. But industry made possible the 'economic independence' of the members of the family – i.e., as wage labourers. In place of the family, Gilman upholds 'marriage': 'although made by us an economic relation, it is not essentially so, and will exist in much higher fulfilment after the economic phase is outgrown.' On a new basis of equality between men and women marriage will become a 'personal union for life of two well-matched individuals'.[119] For both Calhoun and Gilman, wage labour established the potential for a new form of family life based upon the personal freedom of its members.

As the family lost its function as the basic unit of commodity production, the traditional laws and morality that had regulated the conduct of its members were thrown into question. The birth control and divorce movements, among others, demanded that the family's internal relations should be entirely determined by its members. Throughout the nineteenth century the birth rate declined while divorces steadily rose.[120] The birth control movement now promised to liberate women from the tyrannical cycle of reproduction. In the nineteenth century the exclusive purpose of female sexuality was understood to be procreation; doctors commonly advised upper-class women to have intercourse only the five or six times in their lives necessary for conception. With birth control, sexuality promised to become an end in itself rather than

109

serving the social imperative of procreation. Similarly, divorce, the very symbol of marriage freely entered into and freely given up, was attacked by conservatives because it placed the rights of individuals above those of society.[121]

The belief in an internally emancipated family encouraged new conceptions of childhood and of adolescence. In the United States the idealization of childhood and the child-centredness of the family had begun with the rise of industrial capitalism. Ralph Waldo Emerson, for example, commented on a new 'tenderness' that emerged in the period 1820–1840: 'Children had been repressed and kept in the background; now they were considered, cosseted and pampered.'[122] Childhood, in addition to being the period in which the child was shaped to adult (i.e., social) requirements, was coming to be seen as an end in itself. By the 1890s a series of reform movements arose – child study, the kindergarten movement, the Herbartians – that argued that the child's natural fund of spontaneity, inventiveness, and imagination should be respected rather than constricted by 'society'. 'Teaching', wrote Maria Montessori, 'shall be rigorously guided by the principle of limiting to the greatest possible point the active intervention of the educator'.[123] Progressive education, arising partly out of the changing educational requirements of corporate capitalism, similarly sought to liberate the child from adult constraints. G. Stanley Hall, rejecting the traditional view of children's play as preparation for the tasks of later life, stressed the radical disjuncture between the child's world and the adult's.[124]

As childhood came to be understood less and less as preparation for adult society and increasingly as a period of unspoiled virtues opposed to it, the transition from child to adult became problematic. In 1904, in *Adolescence*, the culmination of decades of work, Hall invented the concept of a new zone of life half integrated with and half antagonistic to the adult social order. He described adolescence as the 'passionate stage of life', and assigned to it the qualities of moral idealism and intense emotionality that the Victorians had assigned to upper-class women, isolated within the home. Americans, following Hall, have romanticized and prolonged the period of adolescence, unable to incorporate these qualities into their conception of adult social activity.*

An emphasis on sexuality added a special dimension to the twentieth-century conception of personal life. Sexuality was coming to be understood as the basis of human individuality, the natural life of men and women outside society's domination. As with the study of the child, positivistic science went hand in hand with romantic idealization. Most late nineteenth century studies of sexuality before Freud involved the detailed cataloguing of 'perversions'. On the other hand, Margaret Sanger, exemplar of a frank and scientific attitude toward sex, memorialized Havelock Ellis as follows: 'We owe [to him] our concept of that Kingdom of God within us, that inner world . . . Thanks to him we realise that happiness may be the fruit of an attitude toward life.'[125] Freud's view of human activity as divided between the world of instinctual

---

*ibid., p.339. Here is a characteristic quote from Hall's *Adolescence* (Book 2, p.624): 'Woman at her best never outgrows adolescence as man does, but lingers in, magnifies and glorifies this culminating stage of life with its all-sided interests, its convertibility of emotions, its enthusiasm, and zest for all that is good, beautiful, true and heroic.' A contemporary linking of women and adolescence is found in Meredith Tax, *Woman and Her Mind: The Story of Daily Life*, Cambridge, Mass. 1970, p.2: 'It is in adolescence that we first learn how immensely we are impinged on by the world, and how easily it can destroy us. Our incredibly painful self-consciousness may be exaggerated, but it is based on a true perception of how we are constantly judged, how our very being is assaulted.'

pleasure that is an end in itself (play) and the world of social reality in which activity is shaped by extrinsic purposes (work) is the culmination of all these tendencies.

Finally, and most important, the emergence of personal life was linked to a reformulated view of individuality. It was no longer possible to identify the individual simply with his or her place within the social division of labour. The development of an important zone of personal life cut off from commodity production encouraged the discovery and investigation of the interior or psychological life of men and women. The ideas of consciousness, in anything like our contemporary formulation, and of the unconscious, developed at the end of the nineteenth century. Earlier psychologies had all assumed an isomorphic correspondence between the elements of the mind and the elements of the social and material world. In the early 1880s William James, reflecting the advanced thought of his time, repudiated the view that consciousness was composed of discrete elements that combined like building blocks into complex ideas or associations. Instead, he put forth the idea of the stream of thought, according to which everyone's ideas were uniquely personal and different, ideas and emotions were in constant interaction, and the mind was in dialectical relation with external reality. This new emphasis on introspection, on individual uniqueness, and on the emotions reflected in theory the psychological dimension of the emergence of personal life.

Toward a politics of personal life

In the early twentieth century a large socialist movement existed in the United States, along with a widespread conviction that the United States was heading toward a major social transformation. In this context two groups were strategically placed to raise questions of personal life both as separate concerns and in conjunction with the socialist movement: feminists and young radical intellectuals.

No group experienced the subjective isolation of personal life so deeply as women, trapped as they were within the family, blamed for its egregious faults, or forced to negotiate the limbo between it and the world of wage-labour. As housewives, and particularly as mothers, women became a focus of the modern aspiration for personal happiness. The newly emerged areas of personal life were the housewife's responsibility – in particular childhood, but also sexuality, emotional expression, and the family's pattern of consumption. Far from being a refuge for women the family was a workplace. As Charlotte Gilman pointed out, neither women nor children had any private space within the home; the father alone might have a study.

The new ideologies of personal life encouraged the illusion that women were outside the dominant material processes and class relations of their time. The social responsibility of women for personal life was masked as a return to 'natural' affections, a return dependent upon the historic equation of women with the realm of intuition and sensuality. Lacking an explicit connection to social production, the housewife's labour was viewed as her personal expression. The 'new mother', wrote Havelock Ellis in 1933, 'regards motherhood as a relationship of loving and natural intimacy'. No longer guided 'by obedience to outworn traditions she has learnt how to become the friend of her children'.[126] Later, Benjamin Spock began his child care manual with the hard injunction, 'Trust yourself'.[127] Failures in such labour cannot be salvaged by retreat to yet another private realm.*

---

* Not surprisingly, nervous breakdowns and similar crises around the time of marriage amounted to a social epidemic among educated women in the period of transition to the modern family.

Feminists believed that the way out for women was entry into the world of wage labour. From 1880 to 1910 the number of women working outside the home rose from 2.6 million to 8 million.[128] Educated women entered professions such as teaching, nursing, and social work, which were in large part defined by the new ideologies of personal life; service, melioration, and respect for the rights of others. As Jane Addams pointed out, middle-class women's need to be of use (in her case through social settlements) was based upon a 'subjective necessity': the need of women to link up with the rest of society.[129] Most women, however, became office workers, domestics, or factory operatives. They entered the sphere of commodity production as the rising productivity of labour was leading to declining opportunities for employment. This encouraged the consignment of female employment to the lower-paid and less unionized sectors of the economy: the services where labour was similar to that performed within the home and the production of domestic consumption goods, beginning with textiles in the nineteenth century. The really large-scale entry of women into socialized production has taken place since the 1920s at a time when unemployment and under-employment have become structural features of the capitalist economy. Women's experience as wage labourers was predicated upon and encouraged the idea that their real place was within the home.

Both within industry and within the family the division of labour between men and women was widening drastically at a time when the growth of mass production was eliminating the historic justification ('nature' or economic necessity) for that division. But the creation of a separate sphere of personal life created a new justification. The family, and the subordination of women within it, was necessary to preserve a refuge of spiritual and emotional life against the dehumanization of capitalist society. To a significant extent feminists acquiesced in this conception, and supported the suffrage and female employment as reforms that would humanize public life. One manifestation of this impulse was the genteel women's club, which extended the ideals of domesticity into community life. The major feminist achievement – the suffrage – left the family intact.

Emma Goldman was one of the few feminists who criticized the shrinking of women's politics to the limit of the suffrage. 'Merely external emancipation', she wrote, 'has made of the modern woman an artificial being'. Goldman argued that the emphasis on winning careers for women while ignoring their personal relations had produced 'mere professional automatons'.[130] But Goldman's comments were based upon her sentimentalizing of the traditional domestic relations of the patriarchal family rather than on any attempt to extend the range of politics into the personal sphere.* After winning the suffrage women's politics went into abeyance until the 1960s. During the intervening years women's desire for personal emancipation was expressed through psychoanalysis, bohemia, sexual freedom and other currents of cultural radicalism – currents that accepted personal life as a question outside politics.

The other group whose concern for personal life arose from their ambivalent relation to social production were intellectuals, artists, radicals, and feminists, centred in Greenwich Village, and close to the Socialist Party or the IWW in the early 1900s. The development of a radical intellectual culture reflected the proletarianization of petty bourgeois occupa-

---

* A sentimentalizing that accompanied her belief in free love, personal emancipation and anarchism.

tions such as art, journalism, and teaching, as well as the resistance of young people to life as industrial workers. Early twentieth century radical intellectuals represent a transition between nineteenth-century petty bourgeois individualism and the mass educated labour force of today – which is commonly called the middle class. This group encompassed all those who were able to restrict the role of alienated labour in their lives and to define their major activity outside immediate capitalist production relations: free-lance writers, artists and intellectuals, bohemians and vagabonds, radicals and revolutionaries, 'the men and women without a productive or market function traditional to economic society'.[131]

The American tradition of romantic individualism began with the rise of industrial capitalism in the Jacksonian era. According to Emerson, 'mind had become aware of itself ... the young men were born with knives in their brain, a tendency to introversion, self-dissection, anatomizing of motives'.[132] Transcendentalism, like European romanticism, upheld the self-sufficient individual (or utopian community) against 'society'. But in the early twentieth century radical intellectuals began to combine the romantic defence of individualism with a critique of capitalism itself. Van Wyck Brooks, for example, pointed out that Emerson's 'really equivocal individualism ... asserted the freedom and self-reliance of the spirit [as easily as] of the business man'.[133] Brooks distinguished bourgeois individualism which 'was essentially competitive' from the 'new individualism which finds its gospel in self-expression'. The 'new individualism', he wrote, 'is individualistic only by default'. It is the barrenness of capitalist society that forces the new individualism back into the sectarian world of private pursuits. The initial impulse of individualism is 'filled with an intense, confesed eagerness to identify itself with the life of the whole

116

people'.[134] By offering it only alienated labour and economic acquisitiveness, the United States was 'breeding a race of Hamlets'.[135]

Inspired by feminism, and by psychoanalysis, young intellectuals castigated traditional family life for what Randolph Bourne called its 'blind jealousy toward any assertion of individual ideals'.[136] They anticipated that the new forms of personal life developing in bohemia would spread throughout the population as a result of politics and propaganda. Floyd Dell's *Love in the Machine Age*, which synthesized much of this thought, traced male supremacy to the fact that in 'pre-industrial' society the family was practically the sole economic unit. Women and children had been dependent upon the patriarch for their livelihood. The rise of industry eliminated this dependence but social relations based upon it had persisted. According to Dell, 'patriarchal customs [had] become modern neuroses'. 'Neuroses', Dell explained, were not the result of 'individual shortcomings' but were due 'to our general social-economic backwardness'.[137]

According to Van Wyck Brooks 'the center of gravity in American affairs has shifted wholly from the plane of politics to the plane of psychology and morals'.[138] Therefore a new kind of politics was required – one that addressed itself to the problems of personal life. The young intellectuals were almost universally socialists who rejected any politics that did not encompass a 'program for spiritual and artistic liberation'.[139] They identified art, psychoanalysis, bohemia, and other forms of personal revolt with the impending social revolution. They anticipated no conflict between their individual aspirations and the practical needs of a movement. Dell wrote in his autobiography, 'As a bohemian, I did not ask of myself any regular, practical propaganda duties; my contribution to the revolution would be such truth-telling as I could manage to do

117

. . . as an artist.'[140] According to Brooks, self-assertion had been anti-social so long as it was based upon economic gain. But self-assertion expressed through politics or 'through science, or literature, or mechanics or industry itself' was a 'directly social activity' in which one fulfilled oneself through and with others.[141]

The separation of the personal . . .

Much of the strength of nineteenth-century romantic individualism derived from its association with the French revolution and with currents such as abolitionism in England and America. Similarly, the possibility in the United States of basing a programme of action (a 'politics' broadly conceived) upon the new sphere of personal life was rendered plausible by the vitality and momentum of the socialist and feminist movements. World War I, the Nineteenth Amendment, and the split in the socialist movement after the Russian revolution, however, destroyed these movements and with them the general mood of impending revolution within which individual liberation and social transformation were reconciled. The Bolshevik revolution helped refocus the political attention of European and American socialists exclusively on the question of state power just as 'personal' questions were assuming widespread significance. Following the Russian example the goal of socialism came to be presented purely in terms of economic development. The Communist Party wrote off the pre-World War I currents of personal radicalism as 'petty bourgeois' and rejected as a whole the legacy of romantic individualism and art. Correspondingly, the various ideologies of personal life began to reject socialist politics as 'irrelevant' to the changing needs of the American people. Beginning in the 1920s bohemians looked to France for inspiration while socialists looked to the Soviet Union. A gulf opened between the radicalism of personal liberation and the radicalism of political revolution that remained largely unchallenged until the 1960s.

In the absence of any connection to a concrete social movement the culture that arose on the new terrain of personal life was plunged into subjectivity. Movements such as progressive education, psychoanalysis, and sexual freedom reflected the illusion that personal life could be transformed without a transformation of the mode of production. Lacking any analysis of how capitalism formed personal life, such movements were easily co-opted and integrated into the corporate capitalist system. They have supplied much of the élan in our changing patterns of commodity consumption. Alternatively, these movements resisted 'selling out', but they did so on behalf of the lone individual – the 'genius', the hipster, the beatnik artist. Cut off from production and from the life of the masses of people, cultural radicalism survived in the form of protest movements whose radical content was increasingly esoteric, abstract, and utopian.

Educational reformers around 1900 opposed the child's world of play and imagination to the adult regimen of alienated labour. On this basis reformers criticized traditional education but failed to criticize the capitalist order that produced it. The twentieth century corporate economy demands 'creativity', 'inventiveness', and 'imagination' as constituent elements in the process of production. It requires a more cooperative and socially oriented labour force and a more flexible and diversified curriculum than nineteenth-century capitalism required. Through the work of John Dewey and others the romantic idealization of the child was combined with a programme of social adjustment. Unlike previous reformers Dewey stressed the *continuity* between play and work, and between childhood and society. Respect for the child's innate capabilities was combined with the need to educate the child to what Dewey called a 'socialized disposition'.* In this way the emphasis on the child's spontaneity and freedom lost its critical edge and instead became integrated within the reformed and stratified educational system of corporate capitalism.

The liberating potential of modern art has been similarly dissipated. Since the rise of romanticism the artist has symbolized the free individual who brought to society not the performance of an assigned function but his or her own self.† This image spoke to the situation of proletarianized individuals who felt that their real, inner being was not engaged by their social function. Its peril, however, lay in the artist's unawareness of his or her own social relations and place, as an artist, in the capitalist system of production. With the rise of

---

* Dewey argued that the decline in the productive functions of the family had undermined its educational role. The schools were to fill this vacuum. On the model of the earlier bourgeois family he urged that the school be a collective productive enterprise in which learning proceeded by doing. Lawrence A. Cremin, *The Transformation of the School*, New York 1961, pp.125, 154–57.

†In the romantic tradition the image of the artist or 'genius' as a figure outside the division of labour originally had a democratic aspect. According to Emerson: 'He that is once admitted to the right of reason is made a freeman of the whole estate. What Plato has thought, he may think; what a saint has felt, he may feel.' Ralph Waldo Emerson, 'History', in *The Portable Emerson*, New York 1968, p.139. Similarly Wordsworth asks, 'What is a Poet?' and answers, 'He is a man speaking to men. . . . The Poet thinks and feels in the spirit of human passions. How then can his language differ in any material degree from that of all other men who feel vividly and see clearly?' William Wordsworth, 'Observations Prefixed to "Lyrical Ballads"', in Mark Schorer, Josephine Miles, and Gordon McKenzie, eds., *Criticism: The Foundations of Modern Literary Judgment*, New York 1958.

120

mass-produced art in the twentieth century – publishing, magazines, movies, etc. – the artist's conception of him or herself as a unique individual, a 'genius', became the artist's major defence against proletarianization. The subjectivity of modern art became elitist and mystified. Many currents repudiated romanticism in a search for objective and impersonal disciplines. In either case, rather than symbolizing universal feelings and experience, modern art has become obscurantist and remote from actual human concerns.

Similarly, psychoanalysis has been both integrated into capitalist production and has survived as an esoteric rebellion against it. Originally, psychoanalysis was a time-consuming and expensive treatment restricted to the European and American middle classes. In the form of therapy, counselling, social work, and other institutions this treatment has been extended to large sectors of the working class. The growth of psychotherapy parallels the rise of higher education; both reflect the development of a diversified and educated working class that looks to life outside production for its sense of personal meaning. Once it was integrated into the system of production and administrative control, psychoanalysis could easily be adapted to the prevailing ideology of adjustment, social conformity, and cynical self-confidence. In this context the radical component of Freudian theory appeared to be the instinct theory, the sphere of sexuality and instinctual needs that could not be contained within 'one-dimensional' society. The popularity of psychoanalysis during the 1950s among American intellectuals such as Norman Mailer lay in the idea that the instinctual or sexual component of human life could never be subdued by social imperatives. Similarly, in the early twentieth century, such ideas as vitalism, the life force, the struggle for existence, the *élan vital* and creative evolution were linked to the individual's protest against the existing order. As with the artist, the tradition of psychoanalytic rebellion survives as a defence of the rebel or hipster who stands against the mass.[142]

So long as the realm of personal life was understood as divorced from production, the radicalism to which it gave rise would be forced back upon itself in an ever-narrowing circle of self-concern. The 1920s saw a new literature emerge amid a new social movement – emigration. As capitalism continued to expand, what was there outside capitalism? Novelists like Hemingway contributed to a cult of 'experience' and of the individual. Personal radicalism gravitated toward irrationality, violence, and mystery. From the surrealists through R. D. Laing, a series of movements have arisen to uphold madness as the positive alternative to oppression.

It is in this context perhaps that we can understand the mysterious significance of sexuality in the lives of modern men and women. It is almost as if sexuality has been invested with all the mystery of society itself. Sex has appeared as the ultimately asocial act, the one in which men and women were the most 'natural', in the dark without clothing. As the other world of capitalist society, ignored, denied, and lied about, sexuality stood for the real life of men and women as opposed to the artificial constraints of society. Seen in this way, the most personal and intimate of experiences is, paradoxically, also the most universal and natural.

Yet, sex is also the supremely social act, a human exchange of love and power. As such it is a social relation of capitalist society: male supremacy, authoritarianism, and the need for social connection are integral parts of sexuality. The twentieth-century assertion of sexuality has been an abstract one; it has not included a critique of the social relations of sexuality. The birth control movement, for example, was initially supported by socialists and anarchists because they saw its potential for liberating women from the tyranny of endless reproduction. But no critique of male supremacy was ever sustained within the birth control movement. Instead the movement confined itself to the purely private rights of individuals to choose the sexual life they wished. By 1916 Margaret Sanger was presenting birth control as the solution to working-class misery and as a means of controlling the birth rate of the 'unfit'.[143] A similar fate befell all other forms of sexual radicalism. Sex was 'liberated' (i.e., it became a commodity, an ideology, and a form of 'leisure') but men and women were not. The same dualism applies to Wilhelm Reich, who made the most important effort to integrate sex with politics. Reich accepted genital heterosexuality as a fact of nature and held it up as an ideal against capitalist social relations; he did not subject sexuality to a social critique. Sexuality in our time has been infused with the most complex and intense social meaning, and yet is understood as the realm of pure and private individualism. No wonder that it is in the experience of sex that men and women today so often encounter their own solitude and confusion.

. . . and the political

In nineteenth-century America, personal life entered politics primarily through conservative movements such as prohibition and censorship. Progressives and liberals believed that personal life should simply be left to the individual. Most socialists agreed, adding that a revolution in which the working class took power would free the individual to choose the private life he or she wanted. The socialist respect for individual freedom was important, but it also tended to reinforce the ideology that governs modern personal life – that it is entirely an individual matter. Throughout our century this ideology has given rise to a programme of

123

abstract individualism – personal liberation within capitalist society. And it has encouraged the idea that the oppression of women within the family was not a matter for politics. But this ideology also reflected a profound truth: commodity production had become a restricted part of social life. For socialists to address the questions of personal life, therefore, it was necessary for them to break with the idea that socializing the means of production would revolutionize all society. Or, alternately, socialists had to redefine the meaning of production.

The Communist Party, the dominant force on the left between the Russian revolution and the 1960s, did neither. In regard to women's liberation and the family, as in so many other regards, communists perpetuated the best and deepest nineteenth-century understanding into the transformed conditions of corporate capitalism. As the possibility arose for a society no longer organized around alienated work, the Communist Party defined socialism primarily as a more efficient form of economic development. Beginning in the second half of the 1920s the major public issues the party addressed were support for the Soviet Union and the inability of the capitalist class to provide for economic stability and growth. Communists did not address the question of the purposes of production or the place of production in society as a whole. In the absence of a comprehensive critique of capitalist society on behalf of the alternative of socialism, the Communist Party was unable to develop a sustained public politics concerning personal life.

In the 1920s currents of personal emancipation and cultural radicalism flourished on a larger scale than ever before, but now, and for the first time, almost entirely isolated from the left. Against contemporary currents of free love the party upheld the ideal of sex within marriage. At the same time the Communist Party did pay attention to the transformation of personal relations among its members.[144] Inspired by the Soviet Union, a spartan ideal of female equality and a subculture of 'red weddings' and 'Komsomols' (youth groups) arose. The party stressed the political participation of women and the sharing of housework among party members. However, as the party moved toward a reformist politics in support of existing trade union and 'progressive' struggles, questions of personal life were increasingly seen as irrelevant and even divisive.

The depression nearly destroyed the spontaneous impulse toward personal and cultural radicalism that characterized the teens and twenties. The 1930s was a period of conservative return to traditional values – the nation, rural America, and the family. The rise of new mass media, commercial sports, popular religion, and the psychological and political triumph of the New Deal reinforced the general rallying around 'the American Way of Life'. The family was portrayed as the bulwark of the new community achieved by mass culture. The 1930s witnessed the birth of 'scientific' marriage counselling, a new emphasis on child-rearing, and, in a time of unemployment, the return of women to the home.[145]

The Popular Front policy arose out of the isolated position of the Soviet Union in the face of the rise of fascism. But the communist emphasis on uniting all 'democratic' and 'progressive' tendencies against fascism fed into the conservative nationalism of the 1930s. Communism, proclaimed the party in the 1936 presidential election, is 'Twentieth Century Americanism'. According to Earl Browder, 'all of the immediate measures proposed by the Communists are aimed to protect the home'.[146] The party sought and won a new respectability. As one organizer has written, the 'proletarian garb favored by functionaries was replaced by the business suit'.[147] Since the party did not consider socialism to be an issue during the great depression, communists concentrated more and more on separate reforms and less and less on changing social relations as a whole. The communist emphasis on joining the mainstream of American life is shown in the following remarks from a 1939 *Young Communist League Bulletin* from the University of Wisconsin:

> Some people have the idea that a YCLer is politically minded, that nothing outside of politics means anything. Gosh, no. They have a few simple problems. There is the problem of getting good men on the baseball team this spring, of opposition from other pingpong teams, of dating girls, etc. We go to shows, parties, dances and all that. In short, the YCL and its members are no different from other people except that we believe in dialectical materialism as the solution to all problems.[148]

World War II and the cold war continued and intensified the social conservatism of the 1930s. In the absence of a general struggle for socialism any challenge to prevailing personal or familial mores appeared as an esoteric or sectarian diversion. The decline of American feminism reinforced the party's submersion in traditional and popular social ideals. Partly in response to the isolation of the party in the cold war period, but also because of a 'left turn' after 1945, the party did recreate an internal party culture within which new social relations, including women's equality, were upheld. But this culture prevailed primarily among youth; when people entered the world of work there was great pressure on them to be the same as everyone else and to live like 'real' workers.

The Communist Party believed that it was basing its politics on the needs of the industrial proletariat. In fact it based its politics on those needs only as they were expressed by the trade union movement. The party's greatest effort went

126

into building the trade union movement, but it submerged the public struggle for socialist revolution in this effort. Among industrial workers a critique of family and personal life did not emerge spontaneously. Because communists left unquestioned people's lives as alienated workers they did not see that questions of the family and personal life were integral to every issue they dealt with, from wages and hours, to industrial safety, housing, racism, etc. They left the question of the family, like the question of socialism, for an indefinite and always receding future.

Beginning in the 1920s the number of industrial workers began to decline relative to the overall growth of the working class. Major new sectors developed, particularly after World War II – technical, administrative, and non-manual workers. The number of students grew drastically; between 1940 and 1970 the college population in the United States quintupled.[149] Among these groups the long-suppressed currents of personal radicalism began to re-emerge, first in the late 1950s and then explosively in the 1960s. These tendencies have taken an individualist form that has been easily contained: beatniks, hippies, freaks, communes, consciousness III, rock music, etc. At the same time the new left and the women's movement have raised questions of personal life as political issues – issues related to the organization of society as a whole. The emergence of these movements, along with the black revolt, reflects the exhaustion of the communist tradition and the possibility of a new socialist movement in the United States.

6.
A Note on Psychoanalysis

Psychoanalysis arose at the point of capitalist development at which the family had ceased to be a unit of commodity production, and was increasingly being seen as a refuge from the 'economy' and 'society'. Its subject matter is the internal life of the family and of personal relations abstracted from the mode of production. It comprehends the family as an autonomous institution subject to its own laws of functioning. On the basis of those laws it attempts to construct a science of the family and of personal identity. But psychoanalysis has no theory of how the family is itself socially determined – instead it explains the family in terms of itself. As a result, psychoanalysis cannot distinguish what is universal in the family (a biological unit after all as well as a social one) from what is specific to the family of a particular mode of production. It cannot distinguish what in the human condition is subject to historical transformation and what should be seen as 'civilization and its discontents'. It tends to project the family of developed capitalist society onto all previous history.

The psychoanalytic movement arose along with the possibility of a society in which goods production was no longer the central human activity. Its initial members were intellectuals, doctors, artists, and scientists, who saw themselves as outside the productive process. The needs to which psychoanalysis speaks – for intimacy, self-understanding, sensual and emotional gratification – are needs that have arisen historically. Its mass appeal since World War II reflects the turn of large sectors of the population from a search for private productive property to a search for fulfilment in their personal lives. Psychoanalysis reflects the new social need to be valued for oneself. It invokes the sensual and instinctual life of men and women at a time when their animal energies are no longer given over entirely to production and reproduction. It would moderate asceticism, sexual repression, and self-denial at a time when these traits were becoming less functional to the process of capital accumulation.

Socialists have approached psychoanalysis mainly from two perspectives. Most have viewed it as a rationale for bourgeois unhappiness and a theory of 'individual solutions' – a guide to getting by in capitalist society. This approach tends to perpetuate the exclusion of the family and personal life from politics. Other socialists, including Herbert Marcuse, Juliet Mitchell, Louis Althusser, and Wilhelm Reich, have viewed psychoanalysis as a science whose valid content could be annexed to marxism. But this approach, similarly, reflects the split between commodity production (which marxism studies) and personal life (psychoanalysis). Viewed as separate sciences, marxism and psychoanalysis contain elements that are irreconcilable. Before they can be integrated, important elements in both will have to be critically redefined.

The potential point of contact between marxism and psychoanalysis lies in a conception of the family and of personal life as concrete social institutions, integral to and shaped by the prevailing mode of production. Freud, like Marx, began his study with concrete social behaviour. In contrast to psychiatry, which reduced behaviour to its organic causes, or to philosophical psychology, which posited a separate 'mind' or 'reason', Freud attempted to bring into scientific discussion a new area of social life: 'what is most intimate in mental life, everything that a socially independent person must conceal'.[150] Its most important social content was the family:

> It follows from the nature of the facts which form the history of psychoanalysis that we are obliged to pay as much attention in our case histories to the purely human and social circumstances of our patients as to the somatic data and the symptoms of the disorder. Above all, our interest will be directed toward their family circumstances – and not only, as will be seen later, for the purpose of inquiring into their heredity.[151]

Freud's most important theories, that of the instincts or drives, and that of the unconscious, derive their greatest value when they are situated as part of a theory of the family. At the same time, their ideological character derives from the fact that Freud has no theory of how the family itself has been, and is, continually remade by society.

Freud's theory of the instincts illustrates both the continuity and the contrast between psychoanalysis and marxism. Like Marx, Freud sees human society as part of nature. But unlike Marx, he does not explain how human beings, through history, transform nature (including their own nature, themselves). For Marx, this is accomplished through social labour. The natural or biological condition of human beings – for example, their need for food or shelter – gives rise to forms of social organization and production that transform those conditions. This constant self-transformation of nature constitutes the marxian dialectic. Freud's conception of the instincts potentially extends this dialectic to include our 'inner nature', the instinctual life of men and women.

Before Freud, the instinctual (or natural or animal) component of human life was not generally seen as subject to historical or social modification. Scientists, doctors, and moralists viewed the biological realm as autonomous, subject to laws independent of those that governed social activity. Humanity was understood to be irretrievably divided between lower and higher functions, body and mind, sex and love, organic and functional illnesses, science and morality. To inspire progress, a higher ideal, above and beyond human needs themselves, was necessary. This was tied to political conservatism, for such an ideal could only be realized by an elite free from the imperatives that drove other human beings.[152]

Freud removed the human instincts from the autonomous realm of biology and plunged them into the social world of the family. Freud distinguished between *Instinkt* which is pre-adapted to reality and *Trieb* which is shaped in a definite social context.* Depending upon the influence of this context over time, the instincts express themselves in social activity, fantasy, creativity, etc. Beginning with his early work on hysteria, Freud sought to show how similar mechanisms of instinctual control could express themselves either somatically or psychologically. Before Freud the sexual instinct was thought to have a predetermined object (heterosexuality) and aim (genital sexuality); sexual behaviour that did not conform was 'unnatural'. The sexual drive that Freud describes can take many forms, depending upon the social, biological, and psychological conditions under which it operates.

Freud's thought opens the way for an understanding of the role that instinctual sexuality plays in social life. It makes it possible to talk about transforming our sexual lives as we now talk about transforming our economic and political

---

* Generally translated 'instinct', *Trieb* is Freud's normal usage.

systems. At the same time psychoanalysis considers sexuality only as it takes shape within the family, and considers the family a relatively unchanging social form. As a result, this potential social dimension in Freud's thought has scarcely been explored.

Similarly Freud's theory of the unconscious opens a new dimension to our understanding of society but remains abstract in the absence of a historical view of the family. The Freudian unconscious is created in the course of the 'humanization' of the infant, the transition from the purely neurological state of the newborn to the social state of the child. This process occurs in every society and is different in every society. The social life of the family – acceptance, rejection, presence, absence, feeding, hygiene, etc. – imposes its rhythm and structure upon the child. A later and essential phase of this process is the learning of language, through which the child enters the social universe of discourse: mother, father, I, he, she, me, mine, we ... The psychic life of the child is superseded as we become conscious of our social relations, but persists to shape those relations. The existence of an unconscious is a bio-social necessity: primary instincts and needs must be integrated within a definite social formation. But its content and meaning varies historically according to the actual social relations and ideology contained within the family.[153]

Because the social content of psychoanalysis is restricted to its theory of the family, and because the family is conceived of as a relatively unchanging unit, attempts to develop a broader social theory on the basis of psychoanalysis have failed. Efforts to explain the origins of guilt, the meaning of culture and religion, and the beginning of human society end up as metaphors that project the model of the family onto the screen of history. The absence of a broader

132

social theory, in turn, limits and distorts the psychoanalytic explanation of the family. This can be seen in the theory of the oedipus complex.

It was not the idea of infantile sexuality alone that made the Freudian theory of the family so disquieting. In contrast to the Ruskinesque idyll of the nineteenth-century imagination, the oedipus complex portrays anger, resentment, jealousy, fear, and guilt as normal components of the relations between and among parents and children. Psychoanalysis, far from promising a cure, threatened to take the lid off, which is why, crossing the Atlantic in 1909 to his first major public recognition, Freud remarked ironically, 'We are bringing them – a plague.'

How did this searing and incestuous family life arise? The oedipus complex presents a critical component of the answer: it is within the family that instinctual sexuality is first constrained and socially formed. But how were the social relations of the family, between men and women and between adults and children, themselves formed? To answer this, psychoanalysis is forced back upon itself and explains the social relations of the family in terms of instinctual sexuality. The way out of this circle is through a conception of the family as a historical unit as well as a biological one. Recently social movements have arisen, focusing on the family, which have begun such an analysis. The 'youth revolt' has been expressed theoretically by R. D. Laing, David Cooper, and others, who re-explain the family in terms of the authority relations between adults and young people.[154] And Firestone's attempt to re-explain the oedipus complex in terms of the sexual division of labour reflects the experience of women's liberation.

For socialists, psychoanalysis is critical for including the family within the scope of revolutionary politics. Marxists have rightly pointed out that any society must organize the production of food, clothing, and shelter, but they have forgotten that it must equally organize the sexual and instinctual life of its members, and the process of human reproduction. Under capitalism these related imperatives are carried out separately – socialized commodity production within the factory and domestic labour and sexuality within the family. At present psychoanalysis is the only social theory that gives due weight to the importance of sexuality and reproduction in the organization of society.

Socialists view labour (by which they mean wage labour under capitalism) as the central human activity, and as the practice that distinguishes human from animal life.* This idea has been taken over by feminists who contrast the tasks of sexuality and reproduction to the more 'human' labour performed in the sphere of commodity production. But what distinguishes human from animal life is not labour – it is *conscious* labour. According to Marx:

> A bee puts to shame many an architect in the construction of her cells ... But ... the architect raises his structure in imagination before he erects it in reality ... He not only effects a change of form in the material on which he works, but he also realizes a purpose of his own.[155]

Similarly, what distinguishes human sexuality from animal, and human reproduction from animal, is consciousness

---

* The same distinction between our 'human' and 'animal' activities underlies the puritanism endemic to the socialist movement. Women's liberation has perpetuated this puritanism – for example, by attacking sexual exploitation or pornography without defending some principle of sexual freedom – and has repudiated it – for example, by its defence of homosexuality and masturbation.

too – fantasy, imagination, love, purpose. By this definition the labour performed by the proletariat is no more 'human' than the labour performed by women within the home. We need a movement that will transform both forms of labour consciously, deliberately and in accord with human ends.

Finally, the psychoanalytic emphasis on what has been relatively permanent and unchanging in human experience helps put into perspective the tasks of a socialist movement. History does not begin with capitalism. Many of the social relations that a socialist movement must confront – and specifically male supremacy – ante-date capitalism. Some aspects of male supremacy originate in feudalism, some in slave society, some in taboos of primitive society. As Freud argued in a passage that once again brings out the social content of his theory:

> It seems likely that what are known as materialistic views of history err in underestimating [the force of past traditions]. They brush it aside with the remark that human 'ideologies' are nothing other than the product and superstructure of their contemporary economic conditions. That is true but very probably not the whole truth. Mankind never lives entirely in the present. The past – the tradition of the race and of its people – lives on in the ideologies of the superego, and yields only slowly to the influences of the present and to new changes.[156]

What is important is not to posit male supremacy or any other social relation as arising in a 'state of nature', but to understand that 'ideologies' arise because of definite social conditions (including those of primitive society) and persist in definite social forms. Only in this way can we avoid binding ourselves to some myth of the past and begin to understand that our social relations are subject to our collective intervention. In this sense, a socialist movement confronts not only capitalism, but the entire prehistory of humanity: primitive, feudal, slave, etc. What we face are our own antecedents and the causes of our own development – not some universal dilemma.

Political Conclusions*

What are the political implications of this transformation? First, I believe that this perspective indicates why a
feminist movement emerged independently of the socialist
movement, and some of the strengths, as well as the weaknesses, of that independence. Women are oppressed in new
and particular ways: they have a particular experience which
they must interpret. So long as the socialist movement
focused on the sphere of commodity production it missed a
major dimension of women's oppression. At the same time
feminism itself must be seen historically. Feminism arose out
of this same process of capitalist industrialization – the re-
moval of goods production from the home. It arose first
among bourgeois women in the nineteenth century, appalled
by being isolated in the 'doll's house', and then, more broadly,
in the twentieth century. English and American feminist
movements have often uncritically accepted ideas and conditions which, in fact, had been imposed upon women by the
development of capitalism: for example, a conviction of the
moral superiority of women or the idea of a woman's culture.
It does not seem to me possible for a feminist movement alone
to transcend these origins – even if it is socialist, and even if it
takes as the area of its concern the whole of society from the

---

* The following is an excerpt from a speech delivered at a New
American Movement forum, at Berkeley, California, 13 December
1973.

family to imperialism to the state and so forth, as socialist-feminist movements now do.

More to the point, the tasks required for the liberation of women cannot be accomplished by women alone. Specifically I do not believe that women alone can transform the family. Efforts to do so, such as communes, when they are viewed as political ends in themselves, wind up reproducing the family precisely because they reproduce both its dependence on production, and its isolation from production. The family cannot be transformed except as part of the general transformation and destruction of the capitalist economy. This requires the united efforts of all working people, including housewives.

Second, the development of a separate sphere of personal life means that sections of the modern working class have a real sphere of personal freedom and independence which previous labouring classes did not have, and this sphere has increased as capitalism has developed. This was reflected in the early programmes of radical feminism which put all stress on the self-transformation of personal relations. The programme took the form of demands which women made upon themselves, upon one another, and upon individual men. Communes represent an example of this kind of programme. Also, outside the family, things like 'free schools' or counter-institutions reflect the same tendency. This represents a new element in socialist politics. Traditionally, socialists made demands upon the state or upon the capitalist class, and expected revolution to occur when those demands were denied. In addition, the revolutionary party sought to supply 'services' to the people. But a contemporary revolution will have a greater degree of personal and communal experimentation than a revolution would have had in the United States a century ago. Radical feminism represented an extreme emphasis on this pole. Other feminist tendencies tend to leave in abeyance the problem of developing a programme that men and women could institute by themselves and, instead, to make direct claims upon the state. This is true of much reformist activity and of the demand of wages for housework.

A socialist programme must involve both poles of this dichotomy. The best start toward such a programme that I have seen, insofar as it is focused on the family, is the *Programmatic Manifesto of Housewives in the Neighbourhood*, which comes from the Mariarosa Della Costa branch of the Italian women's movement and which was printed in *Socialist Revolution 9*. Its basic point, and this must be the basic point, is that housework is socially necessary labour. Accordingly it must be shared by the entire community. I quote:

> We affirm all labor hitherto carried out by women, that is: cleaning the house, washing and ironing, sewing, cooking, looking after children, taking care of the old and sick, are forms of labor like any other, which could be carried out equally by men or women and are not of necessity tied to the ghetto of the home.

Hence they call, for example, for 'all cleaning of houses to be carried out by those people, men and women, who wish it to be done'. Similarly they reject what they call 'state ghettos' for the children, the aged and the sick. They call for neighbourhood canteens, neighbourhood laundry services, and neighbourhood nurseries, run and serviced by the people who are themselves involved. This reflects one side of the programme, the self-transformation of social relations. They then write:

> This reorganization and socialization of labor is, in our view, only possible within the revolutionary process. It has revolutionary significance as opposed to capitalist rationalization only to the

extent that a drastic reduction of the workday is achieved, for all men and women, which would allow qualitatively greater possibility of social living. All this means a working week of twenty hours.

That is the other side of the programme, the struggle against the state and the capitalist class. Being able to bring both sides together has a lot to do, it seems to me, with reconciling the so-called 'middle-class' ranks of educated labour with the industrial working class of contemporary capitalism.

Third, this perspective makes it possible to speak of personal life without apologies or hesitations: to give it its due politically, and to prevent it from taking over and submerging political projects, as it will certainly do if it is denied or ignored. Personal life emerges historically in a concrete form: its development can be traced fairly precisely. It is just as real, just as substantial a process as the spread of monopoly capital into the auto industry or the current decline in real wages. Its cause is, in fact, the socialization of production achieved by capital – particularly the reduction in the work week. It represents a new historical space, within which historically new needs have taken shape. It is tied into the mode of production through the labour of women in the home. At the same time it comes cloaked in an ideology that disguises its relationship to the rest of society and that confirms the modern working class in its illusion of freedom and autonomy. Socialists must speak critically of 'personal life' just as we now speak critically of 'the standard of living' or 'the national interest'.

Only socialism can finally transform personal life because only socialism will abolish alienated labour. In this sense, 'personal life', as autonomous life activity, is yet to be created. Under capitalism almost all of our personal needs are restricted to the family. This is what gives the family its resilience, in spite of the constant predictions of its demise, and this also explains its inner torment; it simply cannot meet the pressure of being the only refuge in a brutal society. Socialism carries the promise of diffusing our personal needs throughout the entire society – and particularly throughout the world of work. This is a reintegration of society that could never be accomplished under capitalism because it presumes that the economy will be governed by criteria other than blind, meaningless, quantitative aggrandizement.

A socialist programme for the family should consider all the dimensions of personal life – economic, social, and psychological – and should attempt to relate them. Its governing principle should be the enhancement of personal life through the enhancement of social life. Capitalism is organized so that basic needs are met individually. Psychological needs, such as self-recognition, are met within the family; material needs are similarly satisfied, family by family, through the wage system. But capitalism simultaneously gives rise to needs which cannot be satisfied individually – for example, needs for clean air, sun, open space, planned cities, parks, public transport and communication, and a common culture. The dilemma of the housewife is a classic expression of this contradiction: her family's income may rise, technology may lessen the burden of work, but she remains oppressed because she remains isolated. She needs child care, public restaurants, laundries, canteens, recreation, etc. The prerequisite to realizing the promise of personal life is to abolish its forced separation and isolation.

At the same time, socialists must develop a critical perspective toward personal life. The form that personal needs take in capitalist society tends to be all-engulfing – precisely because they are experienced subjectively. To expect that our personal needs will be met under capitalism, in the form in

141

which they are experienced, is as mistaken as ignoring those needs. For a political movement to foster such an expectation would represent a new form of economism: that is, an uncritical acceptance of social needs immediately as they have been generated within capitalist society. Part of our problem in dealing with these questions is that socialists tend to hold to conservative and inadequate psychological conceptions, according to which human beings are essentially thought and labour. But the human need to love and be loved is as fundamental as the need to work. We need a more tentative and experimental attitude toward emotional life. We should realize that feeling, intuition, and sensation have their own special value, and their own limitations, just as rational thought does, and that the kinds of personalities we've developed, particularly our one-sided emphases on either thought or feeling, are the result of particular forms of historical development.

Finally, a conception of personal life adds a special dimension to a socialist revolution. For the present it is one problem among many – imperialism, racism, political democracy, etc. But in a certain sense it will be longer lasting. If we think ahead, even hundreds of years, long after the entire globe has become socialist, long after the wars between nations and races and sexes, currently raging, have quieted down and become part of history, we can ask, what will then be the tasks facing society? Our own task, the most immediate and urgent one facing us, will then be solved: production will be rationalized and socialized. Labour, distribution, consumption, etc., will be under our purposeful control. What will society then be about? It seems to me that it will then be about some form of personal development, achieved by individuals both through social activity, and alone. This kind of activity will increase as production and its imperatives –

the realm of necessity – occupy a smaller and smaller place in human life.

This somewhat utopian possibility is foreshadowed in the present. Until our own times all human relations were integrated with, and subordinated to, the imperatives of economic production. This was the case in capitalism so long as the self was identified with private property and social life (including the family) with production. But with the socialization of production a split opened between work and life, between the family and the economy, which has given rise to a new idea unrealizable under capitalism: that of human relations and human beings as an end in themselves. It is this idea that gives the family, and such institutions as romantic love or childhood, their unique modern character. As it currently prevails this idea is ideological. As the historian Martin Sklar points out, the contemporary proletariat, having no private property to uphold, upholds the 'self' as an autonomous realm outside society. The idea of 'life-style' expresses this ideology. At the same time this ideology expresses a realistic possibility: that of a society in which the production of necessary goods is a subordinate part of social life and in which the purposes and character of labour are determined by the individual members of society. The ideal of a life no longer dominated by relations of production has an old and elitist history: it has been the province of philosophers, aristocrats, courtiers, mystics, and then in the nineteenth century, artists and intellectuals. In contemporary society it has been achieved in a distorted and mangled form by the entire working class. Socialism will make possible the realization of that ideal on a democratic and universal basis.

References

1. Kate Millett, *Sexual Politics*, New York 1970, p.24.
2. ibid., pp.23–24; other modern pioneering works, which predated the emergence of women's liberation, would include Simone de Beauvoir's *The Second Sex*, New York, 1952, Betty Friedan's *The Feminine Mystique*, New York 1963, and Juliet Mitchell's 'Women: The Longest Revolution', *New Left Review* 40, 1966.
3. Juliet Mitchell, *Women's Estate*, New York 1971, p.83.
4. Shulamith Firestone, *The Dialectic of Sex*, New York 1970, p.149.
5. ibid., pp.36–42.
6. ibid., p.99.
7. ibid., p.84.
8. ibid., pp.87, 90.
9. ibid., p.148.
10. ibid., p.148.
11. ibid., p.156.
12. ibid., pp.167, 172.
13. ibid., p.92.
14. Philippe Ariès, *Centuries of Childhood: A Social History of Family Life*, translated by Robert Baldick, New York 1962.
15. Karl Marx, *Neue Rheinische Zeitung*, 15 December 1848, quoted in C.H.George, 'The Making of the English Bourgeoisie, 1500–1750', *Science and Society*, Winter 1971, p.385.
16. Christopher Hill, *Century of Revolution, 1603–1714*, New York 1961, p.253.
17. Christopher Hill, *Society and Puritanism in Pre-Revolutionary England*, New York 1967, p.449; Marc Bloch, *Feudal Society*, Chicago 1968, pp.123–44.
18. Quoted in Sheldon Wolin, *Politics and Vision*, Boston 1960, p.298.
19. John Locke, *Treatise of Civil Government*, New York 1937, pp.18–19.
20. Lawrence Stone, *The Crisis of the Aristocracy, 1558–1641*, New York 1967, pp.298–301.
21. Hill, *Society and Puritanism*, p.449.

22. Lionel Trilling, *Sincerity and Authenticity*, Cambridge 1972, p.25; Hill, *Century of Revolution*, p.253.

23. Simone de Beauvoir, *The Coming of Age*, New York 1972, pp.178–79.

24. Mary Beard, *Woman as Force in History*, New York 1946, 1971, p.234.

25. Quoted in M.M.Knappen, *Tudor Puritanism*, Chicago 1939, 1970, p.454.

26. George, pp.407–8. In fact, this did not become a legal reality until the middle of the eighteenth century.

27. C.B.Macpherson, *The Political Theory of Possessive Individualism*, London 1967, p.149.

28. Paul Mantoux, *The Industrial Revolution in the 18th Century*, New York 1961, pp.59–68. Maurice Dobb, *Studies in the Development of Capitalism*, New York 1968, pp.143–51.

29. E.P.Thompson, *The Making of the English Working Class*, New York 1963, pp.306–7.

30. *Neil Smelser, Social Change in the Industrial Revolution*, Chicago, 1965, passim.

31. Thompson, pp.359, 368–69.

32. Andrew Ure, *Philosophy of Manufactures* (1835), quoted in Thompson, p.360.

33. By 'society' Rousseau refers to commerce and urban life rather than to the industrialization then occurring in England. Nevertheless, the overall direction of French and English society is similar.

34. *Emile*, London 1966, p.401. Eva Figes, *Patriarchal Attitudes*, New York 1970, points out the importance of Rousseau.

35. Ernst Cassirer, *The Question of Jean-Jacques Rousseau*, Bloomington, Indiana 1967.

36. E.P.Thompson, 'Time, Work-Discipline and Industrial Capitalism', *Past and Present* 38.

37. Wolin, pp.316, 324, 333, 341. The phrase 'solely from the outside' is from Wolin, p.340. The rest are from Bentham.

38. Trilling, pp.39–41, points out that insofar as the vision of a 'good life' existed in the nineteenth century – in Shakespeare's words 'quiet days, fair issue, and long life' – it was an ideal associated with the aristocracy. Material abundance and a willingness to accept pleasure were not part of the outlook of the nineteenth-century bourgeoisie.

39. Ernest Jones, *The Life and Work of Sigmund Freud*, New York 1953, Vol. 1, pp.190–91.

40. Coventry Patmore, 'The Angel in the House', quoted in Walter Houghton, *The Victorian Frame of Mind*, New Haven 1957, p.345.

41. John Ruskin, 'Of Queens Gardens', quoted in Millett, pp.98–99.

42. Thomas Carlyle, *Past and Present*, quoted in Houghton, p.345.

43. Ruskin, quoted in Millett, p.99.

44. S.Ellis, *The Daughters of England*, London 1845, pp.22–23, quoted in J.A. and Olive Banks, *Feminism and Family Planning in Victorian England*, New York 1964, 1972, p.59; see also p.22.

45. Quoted in Millett, p.105.

46. Houghton, p. 347, quoting Charles Kingsley, *Letters and Memories*.

47. Ruth Bloch, 'Sex and the Sexes in 18th Century American Magazines', unpublished manuscript.

48. S.A.Sewall, *Women and the Times We Live In*, quoted in Banks, p.60.

49. Bentham again, quoted in Wolin, p.342.

50. *Mark Rutherford's Deliverance*, Chapter 8, pp.106–7, quoted in Houghton, p.346.

51. Quoted in Houghton, p.347.

52. Shlomo Avineri, *The Social and Political Thought of Karl Marx*, Cambridge 1969, p.90.

53. Percy Bysshe Shelley, *Complete Poetical Works*, London 1881, p.223; Kenneth Neill Cameron, *The Young Shelley: Genesis of a Radical*, New York 1950, p.270.

54. *The Condition of the Working Class in England*, Stanford 1968, p.145.

55. This quotation is from the 1847 *Communist Credo* by Engels, which preceded the Communist Manifesto. Dirk Struik, ed., *Birth of the Communist Manifesto*, New York 1971, p.185.

56. Quoted in Raymond Williams, *Culture and Society*, New York 1958, p. 15.

57. Arnold Hauser, *The Social History of Art*, Vol. 3, New York 1958, pp.53, 81; Williams, 'The Romantic Artist', in *Culture and Society*; Eric Hobsbawm, *The Age of Revolution, 1789–1848*, New York 1964, p.307.

58. E.P.Thompson, *Making of the English Working Class*, passim.

59. William Wordsworth, 'Observations Prefixed to "Lyrical Ballads"', in Mark Schorer, Josephine Miles, and Gordon McKenzie, eds. *Criticism: The Foundations of Modern Literary Judgment*, New York 1958, p.36. Ideas similar to those of the romantics were expressed within evangelical and millenarian groups.

60. Morse Peckham, *The Triumph of Romanticism*, Columbia, S.C., 1970, pp.36–46. Peckham refers to these as 'anti-roles'.

61. Charles Baudelaire, 'The Painter of Modern Life', in Peter Quennell, ed., *The Essence of Laughter*, New York 1956, p.52.

62. Quoted in Williams, *Culture and Society*, p.73.

63. Georg Lukács, *History and Class Consciousness*, Cambridge, Mass., 1972, p.136.

64. Karl Marx, *Pre-Capitalist Economic Formations*, New York 1964, pp.84–85.

65. Jurgen Kuczynski, *The Rise of the Working Class*, New York 1967, p.115.

66. Eric Hobsbawm, *Industry and Empire*, New York 1968, p.73.

67. Stuart B. Ewen, 'Advertising as Social Production', *Radical America*, May 1969, pp.46–47.

68. Il Manifesto, 'Technicians and the Capitalist Division of Labor', *Socialist Revolution 9*, May–June 1972, pp. 66–69. This sense is even more pronounced within bureaucracies.

69. Many services are direct adjuncts of goods production. Further, a large component of all service industries can be resolved into goods production – consider the health industry as an example.

70. James O'Connor, *The Fiscal Crisis of the State*, New York 1973.

71. Gail Parker, ed., *The Oven Birds: American Women on Womanhood, 1820–1920*, New York 1972, pp.4 ff.

72. Christopher Lasch, *The New Radicalism in America, 1889–1963: The Intellectual as a Social Type*.

73. Meredith Tax, *Woman and Her Mind: The Story of Daily Life*, Cambridge, Mass., 1970, pp.7, 17.

74. David Montgomery, *Beyond Equality*, New York 1967, p.28.

75. Selma James and Mariarosa Dalla Costa, *The Power of Women and the Subversion of the Community*, Bristol 1972.

76. Firestone, pp.6, 12.

77. This they shared with the bourgeois thinkers of the period – economics, for example, used to be studied as 'political economy' and 'moral philosophy'.

78. Frank and Fritzie Manuel, *French Utopias*, New York 1966, p.219.

79. Fourier, *Design*, p. 65.

80. In Britain the circle of Shelley, Godwin, and Mary Woolstonecraft represents a related development.

81. Quoted in Nicholas Riasanovsky, *The Teaching of Charles Fourier*, Berkeley 1969, p.216.

82. ibid., p. 149.

83. The first quote is from John Humphrey Noyes, *American Socialisms;* the second from Charles Lane, 'Brook Farm', *Dial,* January 1844; both cited in John Thomas, 'Romantic Reform in America, 1815–1865', *American Quarterly,* Winter 1965, pp.656–81.

84. Actually, of *commercial* capitalism, more developed than industrial capitalism in France, and the sector in which Fourier worked.

85. Frederick Engels, *The Origin of the Family, Private Property and the State* (1884) in Marx and Engels, *Selected Works,* Moscow 1962, Vol. 2, p.326, n. 1. Lack of time prevented him from doing so. See also Marx and Engels, *Selected Correspondence,* Moscow 1965, p.373.

86. *Origin,* p.308. Engels' account is largely based on Lewis Henry Morgan's study of the Iroquois.

87. ibid., p. 240.

88. ibid., p. 209.

89. ibid., p.225.

90. ibid., p.240.

91. ibid., p.252.

92. ibid., p.263.

93. ibid., p.318.

94. ibid., p.240.

95. ibid., p.311.

96. Two excellent and balanced discussions of *The Origin of the Family,* both, I believe, still in manuscript, are Ann J. Lane, 'Women in the Industrial Process: A Critique of Frederick Engels', and Rosalind Delmar, 'Some Comments on Engels' *Origin of the Family'.*

97. This entire paragraph derives from Delmar's article, though her argument is significantly different.

98. Firestone, pp.3–15.

99. Rosa Luxemburg, 'Women's Suffrage and the Class Struggle', in *Selected Political Writings,* edited by Dick Howard, New York 1971, p.220. Luxemburg's purpose in this passage was to point out the absurdity of a society in which surplus value determined social needs, but her argument is that only women's entry into the labour force establishes a basis for socialist response.

100. V.I.Lenin, *On the Emancipation of Women,* Moscow 1968, p.101.

101. Karl Kautsky, *The Class Struggle,* New York 1971, pp.26, 127–29.

102. *On the Emancipation of Women,* p.16, n.

103. Quoted in H. Kent Geiger, *The Family in Soviet Russia,* Cambridge, Mass. 1968, p.77.

104. E.H.Carr, *Socialism in One Country*, Vol. 1, Baltimore 1970, p.39.

105. Leon Trotsky, *Women and the Family*, New York 1970, pp.32–35.

106. Rudolf Schlesinger, ed., *The Family in the USSR*, London 1949, passim.

107. Quoted in Geiger, pp.61–62.

108. ibid., p.71.

109. Firestone, p.248.

110. Birth control teams speak against 'the repeated desire to have at least one son'. Soong Ching Ling, 'Women's Liberation in China', *Peking Review*, 11 February 1972, p.7. For the rest of this paragraph see Laurie Landy, *Women in the Chinese Revolution*, New York n.d., passim; C.K.Yang, *Chinese Communist Society: The Family and the Village*, Cambridge, Mass. 1959, 1968, pp.3–21, 208 ff.; Maria Antonietta Macciocchi, *Daily Life in Revolutionary China*, New York 1972, pp.348–78.

111. Stokely Carmichael, 'Pan-Africanism – Land and Power', *Black Scholar*, November 1969, pp.36–37.

112. These are Mencius's categories. Yang, p.7.

113. Particularly with the 4 May Movement.

114. Franz Schurmann, *Ideology and Organization in Communist China*, Berkeley 1970, pp.423 ff.

115. William Hinton, *Fanshen*, New York 1968; Committee of Concerned Asian Scholars, *China!: Inside the People's Republic*, New York 1972, pp.266–92; Charlotte Bonny Cohen, 'Experiment in Freedom', in Robin Morgan, ed., *Sisterhood is Powerful*, New York 1970, pp.385–420.

116. Landy; Macciocchi, pp.348–78.

117. Mitchell, p.121.

118. W. Arthur Calhoun, *A Social History of the American Family*, Vol. 3, Cleveland 1919, pp.157–58.

119. Charlotte Perkins Gilman, *Women and Economics*, New York 1966, pp.213–16.

120. David Kennedy, *Birth Control in America: The Career of Margaret Sanger*, New Haven, Conn. 1970, p.37, n. 1.

121. William O'Neill, *Divorce in the Progressive Era*, New Haven, Conn. 1967, p.260.

122. Emerson, 'Historic Notes of Life and Letters in New England', in Perry Miller, ed., *The American Transcendentalists*, New York 1957, p.5.

123. Quoted in Elizabeth Lawrence, *The Origins and Growth of Modern Education*, Baltimore 1970, p.331.

124. Dorothy Ross, *G. Stanley Hall: The Psychologist as Prophet*, Chicago 1972. pp.299–300, 307.

125. Margaret Sanger, *Autobiography*, New York 1938, 1971, p.141; see also O'Neill, pp.89–167.

126. Havelock Ellis, *Of Life and Sex*, New York 1922, 1957, p.128.

127. Benjamin Spock, *Baby and Child Care*, New York 1970, p.3.

128. Meta Stern Lilienthal, *From Fireside to Factory*, New York 1916, p.42; Eleanor Flexner, *Century of Struggle*, New York 1971, p. 230.

129. Jane Addams, 'The Subjective Necessity of Social Settlements', in Christopher Lasch, ed., *The Social Thought of Jane Addams*, Indianapolis, Ind. 1965, pp.28–43.

130. Emma Goldman, 'The Tragedy of Women's Emancipation', in Alix Kates Shulman, ed., *Red Emma Speaks*, New York 1972, p.176.

131. Martin J. Sklar, 'On the Proletarian Revolution and the End of Political Economic Society', *Radical America*, May–June 1969.

132. Emerson, pp.5, 7.

133. Brooks, 'America's Coming of Age', in Claire Sprague, ed., *Van Wyck Brooks: The Early Years, A Selection from His Works, 1908–1921*, New York 1968, p.99.

134. Brooks, 'Toward a National Culture', in Sprague, p.190.

135. ibid., p.188.

136. Quoted in Christopher Lasch, *The New Radicalism in America, 1889–1963: The Intellectual as a Social Type*, New York 1965.

137. Floyd Dell, *Love in the Machine Age*, London 1930, pp.5, 404.

138. Brooks, 'America's Coming of Age', in Sprague, p.151.

139. Henry May, *The End of American Innocence*, New York 1969, p.304.

140. Floyd Dell, *Homecoming: An Autobiography*, n.p., n.d., pp.147–48.

141. Brooks, 'America's Coming of Age', in Sprague, p.94.

142. John Judis, 'The Social Meaning of Psychoanalysis', unpublished manuscript.

143. Kennedy, pp.112 ff.

144. Information on the Communist Party from conversation with James Weinstein, June 1973.

145. Warren Susman, ed., *Culture and Commitment, 1929–1945*, New York, 1973, introduction, p.16.

146. Earl Browder, *The People's Front*, New York 1938, p.201.

147. George Blake Charney, *A Long Journey*, Chicago 1968, p.74.

148. Quoted in Hal Draper, 'The Student Movement of the Thirties: A

Political History', in Rita James Simon, ed., *As We Saw the Thirties*, Urbana, Ill. 1967, p.181.

149. Robert Carson, 'Youthful Labor Surplus in Disaccumulationist Capitalism', *Socialist Revolution 9*, p.35.

150. Sigmund Freud, *The Complete Introductory Lectures on Psychoanalysis*, New York 1966, p.18.

151. Sigmund Freud, *Dora: Fragment of an Analysis of a Case of Hysteria*, New York 1969, p.32.

152. O. Mannoni, *Freud*, New York 1971.

153. Louis Althusser, 'Freud and Lacan', in Althusser, *Lenin and Philosophy*, New York 1971, pp.189–220.

154. Mitchell, p.165.

155. Karl Marx, *Capital*, Vol. 1, Moscow 1965, p.178.

156. Freud, *Complete Introductory Lectures*, p.531.

Index